Critical Approaches to Online Learning

CRITICAL PRACTICE IN HIGHER EDUCATION

Dedication

For Lydia and Ned. I hope online is a choice again by the time you read this.

Acknowledgements

My thanks for contributions, support, wisdom and/or permissions are due to John Potter, Sarah Jones, Debbie Holley, Susan Orr, Dave White, Tim McIntyre-Bhatty, Deborah Gabriel, Gail Davies, Anna Feigenbaum, Eva Braune and David Carless.

Critical Approaches to Online Learning

Julian McDougall

Series Editors: Joy Jarvis and Karen Smith

CRITICAL PRACTICE IN HIGHER EDUCATION

First published in 2021 by Critical Publishing Ltd

British Library Cataloguing in Publication Data
A CIP record for this book is available from the British Library

ISBN: 978-1-914171-01-7

This book is also available in the following e-book formats:
EPUB ISBN: 978-1-914171-03-1
Adobe e-book ISBN: 978-1-914171-04-8

Cover design by Out of House Limited
Text design by Greensplash Limited
Project management by Newgen Publishing UK
Printed and bound in Great Britain by 4edge, Essex

Critical Publishing
3 Connaught Road
St Albans
AL3 5RX

www.criticalpublishing.com

Paper from responsible sources

Contents

Meet the author and series editors

Julian McDougall is Professor in Media and Education, Head of the Centre for Excellence in Media Practice and Principal Fellow of Advance HE. He edits *Media Practice and Education*, runs the Professional Doctorate (EdD) in Creative and Media Education at Bournemouth University and convenes the annual International Media Education Summit. In the fields of education, and media/digital literacies, he is the author of a range of over 100 books, articles, chapters and research reports and has provided numerous research projects for external funders, charities and non-profit organisations including the European Union, Arts and Humanities Research Council, Samsung, the United Kingdom Literacy Association, the UK Government Department for Culture, Media and Sport, British Council, ITV and the US Embassy in London. He has given keynote speeches and joined invited expert panels on education, media and digital literacies in over 20 countries.

Joy Jarvis is currently Professor of Educational Practice at the University of Hertfordshire and a UK National Teaching Fellow. She has experience in a wide range of educational contexts and works to create effective learning experiences for students and colleagues. She is particularly interested in the professional learning of those engaged in educational practice in higher education settings and has undertaken a range of projects, working with colleagues locally, nationally and internationally, to develop practice in teaching and leadership of teaching. Joy works with doctoral students exploring aspects of educational practice and encourages them to be adventurous in their methodological approaches and to share their findings in a range of contexts to enable practice change.

 **Karen Smith** is Reader in Higher Education in the School of Education at the University of Hertfordshire. Her research focuses on how higher education policies and practices impact on those who work and study within universities. Karen has worked within educational development and on lecturer development programmes. She holds a Principal Fellowship of the Higher Education Academy and is currently the Director of the University of Hertfordshire's Professional Doctorate in Education. Karen also leads collaborative research and development in her School, where she engages in externally funded research and evaluation and supports the development of scholarly educational practice through practitioner research.

Book summary

Online learning has become an increasing presence in higher education course design, with most courses combining physical real time engagement with asynchronous learning activity. Now, however, there is a greater need for this one-stop guide to critical practice in this area, as we rethink the role of digital in the social practices of university learning and teaching. This book provides a critical and contemporary 'deep dive' into the socio-material, technological and pedagogical practices at work in virtual and digital higher education. Examples are drawn from across and between disciplinary pedagogies with a focus on blended and hybrid approaches. Each chapter gives attention to the pivot to fully online made urgent by Covid-19 but draws on existing best practice from before the pandemic, and looks ahead to the future. This text:

- synthesises the current research into online learning in higher education;

- takes theory into critical practice for online learning in higher education;

- covers learning, teaching and assessment and their dynamic inter-relationship;

- takes a critical approach to social justice and relationships in online spaces.

Introduction

This book was written between 2020 and 2021. It is not intended to be about 'emergency remote' online learning during a global pandemic. At the time of writing, we don't know what the future will look like in the 'new normal'. Covid lockdowns will be a constant background to the writing that follows and many of the references will be to research published during this period, but the critical approaches here relate to online learning as *a way* of doing higher education, not *the only way* for reasons of infection control. Bayne et al (2020, p xix) express the situation very helpfully: '*When distance once again becomes a choice, not a necessity, we will collectively be in a better and more informed position to understand it as a positive principle in many contexts*'.

The hope is that this book, by drawing together a range of research, practice and arguments around online learning in higher education and synthesising it for critical discussion, can combine with leaders' lived experience of online learning during the crisis and will make a contribution to that informed position.

One of the most pressing critical questions about online learning in higher education is this: how can we reconcile theoretical principles of student-centred, collaborative learning from social constructivism with the more instrumental implications of 'delivering' teaching to individuals, separated from each other in space and sometimes time, through computers? There is clearly a presumption here that we *should* and it is not so clear that this is a shared view, so it's a question within a site of conflict from the outset.

How learning is enabled and where we can locate its arrangement on a space–time continuum are at the heart of what we mean by online learning. Is there restricted or open access; what offline relationships are interlinked with the digital engagements; how much surveillance of the virtual activity is happening; is the digital space a supplement to physical interactions or is it 'just this'?

I am not convinced that we need a learning theory which specifically addresses digital technologies as this seems to be a very deterministic way of thinking. For me, learning is fundamentally about people rather than technology. Many of the existing learning theories can inform designing for learning with digital technologies.

(Thomas, 2020, mybrainisopen.net)

Thomas H rather nails it here. The critical approaches in online learning explored and proposed in this book will concur with his assertion. The lines of enquiry will be cast to investigate how people, in online spaces in and around higher education, work with one another to enable learning, generate new knowledge and change the world for the better, in the pursuit of social justice. The approach taken here will neither claim to generate new theories just for the online space nor will this be about 'what works' or how to increase performance against existing metrics. Rather, the project at hand is a *critique* of online learning in higher education and in setting out in that direction, there is an inevitable bias towards the idea of the 'critical', which assumes a deficit alternative.

This opening chapter will offer critique and synthesis of key principles, from the findings of the research relating to the need to teach *through* the screen, the multi-faceted spaces of virtual learning and the pedagogic mindset required. Critical practice and research-informed perspectives will be summarised regarding the 'flipped default' to asynchronous with real time as supplement; dynamic learning and teaching practices shifting static content to agentive and productive enquiry; and the prospect of a critical knowledge exchange with students as partners. The hypothesis that online learning spaces can be productive 'third spaces' if they are charged with creative, productive possibilities, combined with an ethnographic turn in curriculum design, is at stake.

Quick shout out of solidarity to any university colleagues on here who also became academics because they liked reading books and writing essays, and were probably a bit of a geek, and who now find themselves doing the equivalent of hosting a live TV cable channel every day instead.

(@gailfdavies, 25 September 2020)

This tweet caught the eye at the start of the academic year 2020–21 when academics were realising that the 'online pivot' necessitated by the lockdown in the summer was going to be a long-term 'new normal'. As stated, this book won't focus on Covid or treat online learning as a necessary evil during a crisis. However, the 'shock of the new' articulated by Davies is a nice illustration of a key critical question for our consideration here – when students are learning online, are we, their teachers, doing something different; do we become hosts, entertainers even? If the medium is the message, what is the medium; what are we thinking about when we talk about the learning environment? And what does it mean to be the 'host' of learning; are we the medium or is it the meeting?

Space

The UK Higher Education's Quality Assurance Agency (QAA) provides a 'taxonomy for digital learning' (2020). This guidance for higher education staff differentiates online, virtual and digital learning. Online, according to the QAA, is internet-reliant, virtual is similar in engagement level to 'real' and digital is a more neutral category. Blended and hybrid learning fuse timetabled activities with digital 'between times', with the latter usually associated with a higher degree of choice or flexibility. Distance/remote learning are terms used to describe modes of engagement that, whether by choice, design or necessity, are removed from the rest of an institution's 'delivery'. Moving from these terms to a more advisory mode, the taxonomy then distinguishes between the levels of passive, supportive, augmented, interactive and immersive digital experience for students. The final category (immersive) is described thus:

Where digital learning and teaching activities are designed by a provider as the only way in which students will engage, both with the programme and with each other. Students will be required to engage with all the digital activities and will not be offered the opportunity to engage with learning and teaching activities onsite at the provider.

(QAA, 2020, p 12)

The online learning in question in this book *is* the learning. Online *learning* is not about supplementary spaces, such as a virtual learning environment that is used as a repository for materials, or as a more interactive, 'blended' addition to real time, on campus teaching. Going back to the end of the last century, Manovich (1999) observed a shift to an interface model, in media and culture more broadly, and this was enthusiastically and justifiably applied to education, in the sense that the virtual learning environment (VLE) gives students agency over space, time and preference. However, a greater shift is required for the potential of the interface to more profoundly transform how students engage with learning online, described by Bradshaw (2020) as 'ergodic education', whereby the process of choosing our own way through a media narrative is replicated in the student experience of our teaching. Bradshaw's most crucial point, though, which this book can productively return to as a motif as we go forward, is that this ergodic approach is an artful combination of our craft (creating a learning narrative) and the affordance of choice, rather than either at the expense of the other – *'how we might design the "learner journey" and how that tension between narrative and interactivity might be played out'* (2020, blog post).

In their *Manifesto for Teaching Online*, Bayne et al (2020) resist the notion of the teacher as a 'just' facilitator in favour of a series of principles for online *pedagogy*. This critical approach requires us to resist the sense of distance as a deficit; to embrace both a socio-material perspective and a 'troubling' agenda; to pay attention to aesthetics, authorship and the longevity of digital work; to call out complicity with the instrumentalisation of education in online spaces; and to pay (critical) attention to surveillance, algorithms and analytics. The critical approaches taken forward in this book and the manifesto intersect. The argument posited here will be that agentive online learning is possible when we replace thinking about the campus and online as second and third spaces with only 'the space' and then put our efforts into dynamic relations within it, and with it. For Bayne et al, in what amounts to a differently nuanced version of the same argument, there is a campus, but it consists of us:

We are the campus was previously a call from the margins by students and teachers working in geospatially distanced networks. During the global Covid-19 lockdown it became a description of the operational mode of the majority.

(Bayne et al, 2020, p xviii)

We need a conceptual framework going forward that will enable us to think about online learning, and our roles as teachers in virtual spaces, both critically and positively. And we must acknowledge that we already do this every day – none of us are uncritical about three-hour lectures, or 'death by PowerPoint'; the neoliberal politics of lecture capture and advance uploads of our material or the socio-cultural dynamics of the seminar room; assessment design; the failure of our pedagogies to address diversity; and the habitus clash faced by first-generation students. So, the work at hand here is to carry those critical questions about all higher education teaching and learning into the virtual spaces. We need to see the opportunities in the online learning space for more inclusive ways of being in the university. There is absolutely no doubt that these chances to make things better are right here, right now. But we must also be critical, and theorise the learning contexts we produce, most fundamentally placing ourselves at the heart of the situation as teachers, the people who, albeit in a more co-creative, negotiated 'third space', create the possibilities for learning.

The emerging time and space continuum along which we locate our practice in the online learning environments available to us is partly a matter of professional judgement but partly, and often, institutionalised. As educational practitioners we are making decisions within structure and agency dynamics – how do we timetable learning online; what platform? We make choices within a mixed economy – recording 'content' for students to access in their own time; real-time meetings; forum discussions; breakout activities in smaller groups. Again, we make these decisions on campus, but the most profound difference is probably that we timetable first, think later. Now, we can flip that to an extent; but back to the time and space framework.

We are usually encouraged to distinguish between synchronous (happening at the same time for everyone) and asynchronous; between fully online, blended and hybrid. Understood in this way, blended is usually describing a combination of online and campus learning, while hybrid means some of us are in the room and some of us are on a screen. With these ways of working, students generally end up in the room or on a screen for reasons of geography or study context, for example, part-time students either in work or with parental or caring responsibilities, as opposed to because they are able to enable a learning preference. Where such an agentive choice is on offer, this is described as 'flexible' learning.

It looks like a safe bet to predict that blended learning will be the 'new normal'. The pandemic has forced the issue of how the blend might work for different cohorts and different disciplines, so it is difficult to foresee a return to online learning as a supplement to campus as default, wholesale. For this reason, spending more time on blended than the other sub-genres here is useful. Baume and Brown (2017) focus us on the key critical question, what are the ingredients being blended, discouraging us from thinking of the blend as just a mix:

Soon, there will only be learning, using a rich range of tools and resources. We won't call it blended any more. But, for now ... blended learning increases the range of forms of learning open to students, as well as helping students to become more versatile learners. Blended learning draws attention to the idea of investment – investment in course design, investment in the development and selection and learning of resources.

(pp 2–3)

Gilly Salmon's Five Stage model (2013) for blended learning is widely recommended by many practitioners, including Baume and Brown, for taking learning designers through reflection on challenges for students in access, engagement and motivation in online learning contexts; facilitating the building of a 'microcommunity' with support and scaffolding (as opposed to a free-range peer-to-peer space); moving on to group dynamics for knowledge exchange, again with the tutor as a facilitator, into the application of constructivist design principles into the blended learning space and finally, the development stage, where confidence is secure. Salmon uses a con-struction site metaphor, with the teacher as an e-moderator 'foreman' and the blend as a kind of cement mixer.

These genres are reasonable categorical devices and they certainly offer university teachers a coherent transition language into thinking about how we might do learning differently with the internet. But for our purposes in this book, we need a language that can integrate our critical questions about learning into the way we think and talk about online spaces.

Through the connections they make possible, media help shape the present, but always on the foundations of the past.

(Couldry, 2019, pp 30–1)

This is an accepted observation on media and technological transitions, as we move from one form of situated, social literacy to another, from one stage in media and culture to the next. This is as true of the shift to online teaching as it is of the emergence of Netflix. Couldry's framework for thinking about the role of media in our lives provides five aspects – connecting, representing, imagining, sharing and governing. These elements form the mediated social order but, crucially, they are relational adjectives. The social order is constructed through our relations with media and with ourselves through media, our *mediated* relations.

The online learning space is, then, a relational environment but it can be more or less charged with productive possibilities for critical pedagogy. Stommel, Friend and Morris apply the thinking of Giroux and Deleuze to suggest a set of criteria for challenging what goes on in the online space with critical rigour. How engaged is the enquiry; how critical are we of the tools we are using while we use them; how curious is the digital scholarship; how derivative are we in our awareness of sources; and, another intersection with this book, how dynamic are the practices – is the learning and teaching 'framed but emergent' (Stommel et al, 2020, p 223)?

Critical questions for practice

The late Tony Benn (2010) posed these five simple questions to anyone in power:

» *What power have you got?*

» *How did you get it?*

» *In whose interests do you exercise it?*

» *To whom are you accountable?*

» *How do we get rid of you?*

In an online learning environment, these questions are more complicated than in a lecture theatre or seminar room as the power is exercised through a network of institutional, academic, hierarchical and techno-corporate actors, tools and practices. When we are using 'ed-tech' with students, we need to talk to them about ownership of the platform, the data they are asked to share and how we, as teachers, intend to allow it to mediate what we do. More labour-intensive it might be, taking us beyond facilitating online learning in our disciplines, but this reflexive layer, the ongoing deconstruction of the conditions of possibility for what we are doing, and expecting, is essential for avoiding the illusion of virtual learning spaces as more neutral and open than the campus:

There is a paradox here. Once. The imaginative power of media – for example, the nineteenth century novel – was used to reduce the opacity of the social world, to make its vast complexity more manageable by uncovering patterns. But today the newly unleashed imaginative power of algorithmic processes is increasing the social world's opacity, at least to human beings on the receiving end of algorithmic decision-making.

(Couldry, 2019, p 79)

People

Tony Benn's questions are personal and political, when related to learning in higher education. They do something to our professional identities. We choose to work for universities, but when we teach online, but still 'for' the university, which also exists as a physical institution, we are immersed in a more complex network, between us, students, the university, the platform, other digital tools that are owned by companies, and depending on how we are doing things, an extended, secondary audience we aren't in control of. How we feel about this is emotive, and important. In her extensive ethnographic research over two projects with school students in home contexts (2016, with Sefton-Green) and parents (with Blum-Ross, 2020) Sonia Livingstone provided empirical evidence of the complexity of participants' relationships with technology and education, describing how those engagements tend to crystallise broader tensions arising from being a student or parent in the digital age, negotiating risks, opportunities, values and responsibilities. With parents, specifically, three 'genres' of response to digital learning emerged – embracing, balancing and resisting – and, perhaps surprisingly, these generic reactions intersected social class.

It is highly likely that the same is true of university lecturers' responses to the rapid response 'pivot' to online teaching during the Covid lockdown that 'forced the issue' of teaching on screen just as it did for digital parenting.

Transitioning from offline to online teaching and learning has long been found by its earliest researchers and exponents to be complex, problematic and evolutionary, though it can be done by managing the unrealistic expectations that you will be doing substantially the same thing with time, space and material artefacts as you did in face-to-face teaching.

(Williamson et al, 2020, pp 107–14)

Critical questions for practice

Taking a step back to clarify the issue that was, or is being, forced, a conceptual framing consisting of five key questions can be reasonably extrapolated from the plethora of 'grey literature' blog posts, webinar discussions and presentations in circulation during 2020, mapped onto the field of peer-reviewed research into online pedagogies, 'pre-Covid'. These are questions to consider for your own practice, in your own setting.

» How do you teach through the screen, not to the screen? Your teaching space is now a multiplicity of places; a different space, maybe a third space.

» How do you make this more than a pivot? Mindset – forget you have a campus, think about how the campus limits what you do with your students. Shift to *open* education?

» How do you flip the default to asynchronous, real time as supplement – a *'basket of time'*?

» How can you enable dynamic practices, so the direction of flow is not about static content being delivered but about open, agentive and productive spaces for both learners and educators?

» How do you embrace a critical pedagogy of the inexpert, porous expertise, of real co-creation, of learning design? We 'own' the curriculum but not the social practices of teaching and learning; if we ever did.

This 'seize the moment' framing, in turn, intersects with another powerful strand of constructivist university pedagogy from recent years, the interest in 'co-creation' and 'students as partners' (see Bovill, 2020). This meeting point identifies virtual learning environments as potential 'third spaces'. As such spaces are characterised by part-nership and reciprocation between students and academics, the rich possibilities for online learning to be progressive and transgressive (of hierarchies) are obvious. The equation can be described as Third Space (Bhabha, 1994; Gutiérrez, 2008) + Critical Pedagogy (Freire, 1970, 1973; Giroux, 1988; hooks, 1994; Gabriel, 2020) + Students as Partners (Kehler et al, 2017; Hawley et al, 2019) + Virtual Learning. Another four key questions can be added now.

1 Do third spaces *require* negotiation and flattening of hierarchies + embracing different forms of knowledge?

2 How can this be achieved through curational, negotiated, reflexive and interdisciplinary forms of pedagogy?

3 Can online learning spaces only be *third* spaces if they are charged with creative, productive possibilities, combined with an 'ethnographic turn' in pedagogy?

4 If we agree that *'Educational environments should be spaces that facilitate engaged, critical and empowered thinking & action that aim to address societal issues'* (Gabriel, 2019, p 1460), then, can this Covid-imposed 'pivot' to online teaching be an opportunity for us to make these spaces, to decolonise the university (Thomas and Jivraj, 2020)? Or is this a problematic appropriation?

Neil Selwyn is an important critical agent in this field. Back in 2016, relatively recently in other areas of education but much longer ago in the relative timescale of technology, he asked a series of critical sub-questions around the merits of technology for education, set against its problems. How democratic, how personal, how commercial, how different, for better or worse and what values?

Surely, an over-riding concern for the collective rather than the individual is the only way in which technology can be reckoned honestly to be 'good' for education?

(Selwyn, 2016, p 160)

Five years on, and with the sharpened focus on all this that a global pandemic brings into play, the critical questions for practice are extensions and nuanced applications of the above.

Critical questions for practice

» How do cultural meanings circulate in online learning; how are they produced and what might this mean for higher education?

» Who is the 'we' in the space?

⟶

» How do humans, technology and platforms work together in space and how do we humans, with machines and no-human things, offer up possibilities for creative pedagogical practices?

» Which learning theories that already exist can helpfully converge these technological, cultural and pedagogical practices in the socio-material contexts of learners, their habitus and ways of being students with others in the (virtual) world?

» To what extent does this online learning improve the lives of the many, not the few?

Critical issues

The 'third space'

Whether online learning is automatically a 'third space' has been the subject of extensive enquiry (Potter and McDougall, 2016). Such a space is in between the first space of home, community, the personal lifeworld and the second space of school, university and work. The third space is where things are productively exchanged between them, so learning develops out of a meeting point between formal education and lived experience. From Bhabha (1994), 'third space' is a way of defining communication both as the production of meaning and, more importantly perhaps, as a complex act of 'cultural performance'. For Bhabha the space is metaphorical, built into the cultural performance of communication, bounded by institutions and social strategies, always contingent and in an ideologically bound context. Gutierrez reimagined the third space as a way to think about the social actors in a given setting, their autobiographical and temporal specificities and how these could be accounted for in the design of an emancipatory form of educational experience. She wrote about how the design for learning in the third space could resist the standard binaries of home and school, taking into account the lived experience of movement and changes to context. Traditional, earlier operating frameworks of home and school were described as 'deficit portraits' which merely compelled *educators to fix communities and their members so that they match normative views and practices*' (Gutierrez, 2008, pp 148–64).

For those of us concerned with online education practice as a site for negotiated pedagogy, the central challenge is in defining and operationalising its relationship to this third space. Under what conditions can third spaces challenge accepted orthodoxies and pedagogies?

Claims are sometimes made for virtual, screen spaces as 'third spaces' in and of themselves where newer forms of pedagogy might be possible. This risks privileging online learning as inherently dynamic, authentic and easily negotiated, whereas:

Space and place are seen as relational and dynamic, not as fixed and unchanging. Space and place are socially produced, and hence, can be contested, reimagined, and remade. In bringing space and place into the frame of literacy studies we see a subtle shift – a rebalancing of the semiotic with the materiality of lived, embodied and situated experience.

(Mills and Comber, 2013, p 412)

Devices and screens are part of the material world, alongside their owners and users. The third space is also subject to certain conditions and social relations. Seeing the virtual itself as an uncontested source of free-thinking, learner-centred experience in education is not a tenable position, ignoring, as it does, the material circumstances inherent in producing the interaction, the economic imperatives of screen ownership or the political engagements in the (re)production and (re)-imagining of the world onscreen. Instead, the social and pedagogical arrangements of third spaces are such that the real and virtual come together and that the potential for social action in the world is dictated by more complex and pedagogically ambitious designs than may be possible in performative and static systems which, as we have already noted, do not admit the notion that learning is 'dynamic'.

Teaching in and through media – our computers, screens and speakers, ring lights and web-cams, with networked connections to one another – is profoundly relational and is about much more than a set of different ways of arranging learning in different configurations of space and time. It is always-already 'blended' and the kinds of online learning we attend to here will always be flexible, but we will dispense with notions of hybridity, as used to describe on and off campus, because the starting point here will be to challenge the perception that the campus or the university is a place somewhere else that our relational pedagogies on and through the screen, in the network, are a supplement to the 'real thing'. To do this we need to be able to talk critically about, to theorise, how we work with students in the online space and to do that the model needs to enable us to think about it from this point as, just, *the* space. And in *the* space, how do we develop critical pedagogies that combine social justice and decolonising principles with our new mediated relations?

If facilitating opportunities for students to *connect* and *share* in virtual spaces are new 'uses of literacy' (Hoggart, 1957; Bennett et al, 2020), then how do we make use of all this to *imagine* new dynamics of learning for our critical practices – new, potentially radical ways to *represent* ideas about the world and knowledge of it – while remaining attentive to the uses of these new learning literacies on us, and our students, in the form of data harvesting and surveillance – new modes of *governing* what we do in education?

Critical Digital Pedagogy is the way we treat one another.

(Stommel et al, 2020, Introduction, para 3)

We are moving away here from genres, categories or taxonomies that describe configurations of time, space and choice – asynchronous, flexible, hybrid – towards a way of critiquing what happens in *THE* space. The critical theories of education that we need to give us the language with which to construct and problematise *the* space are not new or born out of the digital pivot, but rather the contemporary application of the political constructivism of Paulo Freire, bell hooks, Henry Giroux, Deborah Gabriel and the 'third space' scholarship of Guttierez and Bhabha. Rather, for the development of the ideas in this book, for now, to apply across the chapters, the intention is to keep sharp the focus of the necessary *critical* lens so the gaze is never *only* on pedagogy or the digital but always on both.

Dynamics

The equation is the sum of these parts – online learning combined with critical pedagogy – is always-already a third space but a reflexive layer is provided by relational practices which enable students to imagine. They imagine, with the help of both the teacher and the digital tools and networks, how their learning can be done in the space in order to change the world through the redistribution of power. This is online learning as activism and as learning is theorised 'from within', while it is happening, by those who are both its recipients and agentive co-designers; it is a connected, social and empathetic exercise in *praxis*. In previous work, the distinguishing feature of third spaces that helps us think about the differences between spaces where such agentive negotiations are not only possible but the modus operandi of pedagogy and learning and the more common, static, 'top down' forms of the educational encounter has emerged as *dynamic*. Dynamic learning spaces are those where the ideological, contingent and contextual nature of education itself is transparent and the work of teaching and learning is reclamation and redistribution.

This book is going to think about this space as a singular 'given' – so how is THE (dynamic) space any different because it is online or virtual? Aren't these critical pedagogies the same in the campus seminar room, art studio, laboratory or work placement, within bricks and mortar? Yes, but the critical approaches here are about how the digital space might more immediately disrupt 'offline' hierarchies and how the incorporation of learners' 'first space' skills and dispositions arising out of practices that are representative of wider culture and lived experience is not only possible but necessary for the thing to work. THE space is also more obviously 'socio-material' and brings post-human pedagogical methodologies to the foreground and such direct attention to how epistemological meaning is made through interactions. These reciprocal 'knowledge exchanges' between learners and teachers, artefacts, bodies, machines and spaces and students' lived experiences in wider culture should oblige an intersectional awareness, the possibility at least of transforming the space so that its occupants can work (from within) as allies in decentring learning.

Allies for social justice recognize the interconnectedness of oppressive structures and work in partnership with marginalized persons toward building social justice coalitions. They aspire to move beyond individual acts and direct attention to oppressive processes and systems. Their pursuit is not merely to help oppressed persons but to create a socially just world.

(Patton and Bondi, 2015, cited in Gabriel with McDougall, 2020, pp 168–9)

Pedagogic and social learning practices in the digital age are an assemblage of bodies, space, artefacts, systems and the curational, mediated performance of learning. Sociomateriality, (im)materiality and fractionality (Dezuanni, 2015; Burnett and Merchant, 2014) offer a theoretical language, in dialogue with the aforementioned theories of learning associated with a 'constructivist' education. These developments, in turn, require a methodological thinking, an ethnographic turn in pedagogy, with educational actors telling stories of artefactual versions of socio-materiality, layered with aspects of actor-network theory (Latour, 2005; Law, 2004).

To think of activity in the space as dynamic is to see what we are doing as synchronic, inclusive of situated learning practices, and also diachronic, to look for emergence as a 'baked in' principle. The critical approaches here develop from a cultural per-spective, not a technological standpoint. This is crucial because it is clear that 'ed-tech' solutions do little to situate learners in their lived, mediated cultures. Rather, such instrumental 'tools', allied to big data and algorithms, reinforce performative and profoundly untheorised rhetoric in neoliberal systems in which students are not only measured but become the measure itself. Just as there is an autonomous model of knowledge by which acquisition is assumed to confer status, so there is an autonomous version of the apparently neutral 'uses' of technology in circulation in the marketplace of higher education. Online learning, mediated through technology, is ideological, rather than neutral, being always-already within both socio-material culture and lived experience.

Summary

The book moves on to ask critical questions for practice in higher education with regard to notions of the virtual – how to design assessment for online learning; the opportunities for, and challenges to, the project of decolonising curriculum in online domains; and the role of online learning in our uncertain futures – this establishing chapter has discussed:

- the complex relations between time and space in remote, blended, asynchronous and real-time learning design;

- the equally nuanced and highly situated interaction between human, social and material elements of what we think about when we talk about online learning.

Useful texts

Quality Assurance Agency (2020) *Building a Taxonomy for Digital Learning*. [online] Available at: www.qaa.ac.uk/docs/qaa/guidance/building-a-taxonomy-for-digital-learning.pdf (accessed 2 June 2021).

Sector guidance from the benchmark providers for UK universities. The taxonomy's objective is to provide a 'common language to describe digital approaches to programme delivery'. Clearly the notion of 'delivery' is open to critical questioning, whether online or on campus.

Bayne, S et al (2020) *The Manifesto for Teaching Online*. Cambridge, MA: MIT Press.

Self-explanatory, but note the emphasis on teaching; this collection resists the notion of the teacher as 'just' a facilitator of learning and is also attentive to progressive possibilities within institutional imperatives.

Gabriel, D (2020) *Transforming the Ivory Tower: Models for Gender Equality and Social Justice*. London: UCL IoE Press/Trentham Books.

A series of case studies from scholar-activists, speaks directly to White privilege in the academy and the appropriation of acts of resistance by women of colour. Includes a '3D curriculum' strategy – diversity, democracy, decolonisation. Not about online learning but essential for a critical understanding of the virtual environment as a White space unless configured for anti-racist objectives.

Stommel, J, Friend, C and Morris, S (eds) (2020) *Critical Digital Pedagogy: A Collection*. Washington, DC: Hybrid Pedagogy Inc. [online] Available at: https://hybridpedagogy.org/ (accessed 2 June 2021).

Brings together pedagogic practice from the critical tradition in contemporary contexts with specifically digital applications. Suggests the pandemic sets up a fundamental contest between 'ed-tech' solutions and online education to cultivate 'caring forms of sociality'.

Williamson, B, Eynon, R and Potter, J (2020) Pandemic Politics, Pedagogies and Practices: Digital Technologies and Distance Education during the Coronavirus Emergency. *Learning, Media and Technology*, 45(2): 107–14.

First on the scene, peer-reviewed research-wise, during lockdown. Raises critical cautions against simplistic and opportunistic claims that educational technologies are a ready-made remedy for the current crisis and calls for future research to examine the effects and consequences of the expansion and embedding of digital technologies and media in education systems, institutions and practices across the world, during and post-pandemic.

Introduction

This chapter offers a critical mapping of the idea of a digital pedagogy framework for the sector to the cultural politics of social practices in higher education. Does the streamlining of 'content' for virtual learning enable a rethinking of priorities for more student-centred activity? In teaching and learning online, do we move into more relational and engage 'ways of being' and working together with students as partners in higher education?

We need to reframe the offering and help our academics become more agile. There is still this idea that online is second best. The joy of online and blended learning – which is about digital co-creation and expanding our horizons – hasn't really come yet.

(Holley: Jisc, 2020a)

What happens in an engineering lab or a TV studio can't be replicated online in the same way – but if we think creatively, we can develop learning spaces that allow students to be expressive, active, and engaged.

(Jones: Jisc, 2020a)

These two statements, from a Jisc Digifest panel in late 2020 on 'Building a Better Future', set up the intersection between academics' attitudes to co-creation: the design of new learning spaces and what higher education ought to be for students, or how they can be in higher education and how the space can be designed to make it so for them.

Raymond Williams (1963) accounted for the ways that culture as an 'ideal' is cultivated through education and social 'signifying practices' and described the pursuit of an egalitarian, democratic social mobility through such cultivation as 'The Long Revolution'. Bollmer (2018) used Williams' frame of reference to theorise digital cultures and specifically the differential and relational politics of digital space and time, reminding us therein of the political relation between digital media and culture, a state of 'infrastructuralism'.

The key critical question is about the tension between co-creation in virtual spaces framed by a (neoliberal) discourse of employability and co-creation in virtual spaces driven by more radical pedagogies, open learning, 'Teach Outs' and fluid knowledge repertoires.

```
Critical question for practice

  »  How can you use the online space to positively move away from and beyond
     the 'habitus clash' which students often experience on campus?
```

It is important to unpack some terms of reference here.

Virtual spaces

The use of this term in this chapter does not imply a neat separation between the attempt to replicate real time and space, for example of virtual seminar which is the same length and time as the 'real thing', from online learning which takes place over several days or weeks. Instead, virtual space is understood here as a space that can be moved around, a space in which a student can interact in various ways. Virtual spaces are *experienced*, through immersion and embodiment, but they are not necessarily experienced by people at the same time. Sarah Jones is one of the most prominent academics in the field of virtual reality education and she puts it this way:

I look to building experiences that allow for immersion, using whatever technology I can get my hands on. I am working with ideas of multi-sensory VR to enhance presence in an environment. My approach is based on mobile global collaborative learning.

(Virti, 2020; see also Jones et al, 2022)

Co-creation as relational practice

There is both an institutional discourse and an academic field relating to students and their lecturers working together in new forms of partnership to generate knowledge and create new intersections. Arguably, online and virtual spaces for learning offer particularly rich affordances for more curational, negotiated, reflexive, and inter-disciplinary forms of pedagogy. In this fusion of pedagogic intentions with technological possibilities, there can be a productive convergence of third space and socio-cultural and liminal partnership contexts (Jensen and Bennett, 2016; Hawley et al, 2019). In this way, the threshold concept of student partnership (see Cook-Sather, 2014) can be developed to include the idea of the third space more easily in virtual contexts where both staff and students are trying something new. Activities such as co-creating curricula, conducting joint research, or developing reflexive modules about learning and teaching have the potential to allow students to exert agency and have their voices genuinely heard, and these relational practices are, the evidence so far suggests, easier to generate when academics are operating in new territory with our own roles reconfigured to encompass our own learning 'on the job' in situ. But in the longer term, technology-enabled ways of being in partnership must be more than superficial experiments in co-creation so as to genuinely address issues of social justice, participatory pedagogy and the valuing of the social and cultural capital of all learners in educational settings. Thinking about online higher education as relational in this way obliges us to consider not only the design of learning in virtual spaces but also its ethics (see Arndt et al, 2020).

Neoliberal discourse

Neoliberalism is not a historical fact. It is, rather, a critical way of understanding higher policy in the era of fees; the deregulation of university status and taught degree awarding powers; and the broad principles of market competition driving university strategy:

Neoliberalism is in the first instance a theory of political economic practices that proposes that human well-being can best be advanced by liberating individual entre-preneurial freedoms and skills within an institutional framework characterized by strong private property rights, free markets, and free trade. The role of the state is to create and preserve an institutional framework appropriate to such practices.

(Harvey, 2005, p 2; see also Mayer, 2021)

Neoliberal *discourse* is an articulation, as neutral, common-sense or inevitable, of such an economic modality, whereby education is to be judged on its delivery of graduates to the economy through their 'employability'. The online space can thus be utilised to better connect students to employers, to set up virtual clients, to enhance the impact of university learning on the worlds of science, technology and business, on sectors in the 'knowledge economy'. As such, when we can see that if this way of thinking about higher education is framing or providing a logic for learning in virtual spaces, we will observe an obvious tension with objectives for online learning which seek to resist or 'reclaim' university learning and teaching for either an autonomous modality (knowledge and learning as an end in itself; or for critical thinking) or to actively challenge hierarchies. Whether transformative learning of this kind is even possible within the 'neoliberal university' is the subject of debate:

The neoliberal agenda in higher education has transformed the ways in which students approach their learning. But where students' perceptions and experiences of higher education have been transformed through transformative education, in particular by understanding the ways in which the neoliberal agenda drives the commodification of education, it is possible to reimagine the sector.

(Mayer, 2021, p 3)

Radical pedagogies

These were described in the opening chapter, but by way of a re-set, returning to the contribution made by bell hooks' *Teaching to Transgress: Education as the Practice of Freedom* (1994) as a source text is efficacious (see also Freire, 1970, 1973; Giroux, 1988). We might reasonably conclude that to see education as transgression, as primarily about change and the reduction of inequality, enabling learning to challenge power should not be such a 'radical' idea. But clearly it is very different to the idea that education is about students gaining knowledge 'as it is' and using that knowledge to contribute to the social system and economy, also 'as it is'. The important thing here, for our critical questioning, is that both ways of seeing education claim the virtual space as an opportunity to do things both differently and better. One example is the development of open learning in virtual spaces. This can be seen to break free from insulated, closed walls around modules and programmes so that anyone can join a class and students can take part in rich dialogues across space and time. But at the same time, both massive open online courses (MOOCs) and smaller-scale open learning environments often serve the market logics of institutions and reinforce the value of performative metrics: '*Teach Out to Cash In*', perhaps.

Knowledge repertoires

What is a 'fluid knowledge repertoire', as referred to above? It is important to understand this before going on to judge online learning in higher education for its ability to integrate such a thing. Really, it is a simple shift to thinking about knowledge as dynamic and existing across a set of varied performances, so we perform knowledge from a 'mixed bag' of things we have learned and are learning, as opposed to just receiving it or demonstrating it in a more fixed, static way. Thinking about knowledge and knowing in terms of repertories is especially useful when looking at online learning as it requires us to see knowledge as moving across and between digital and nondigital, offline and online, thinking of learning as lived, so we need to:

fold in digital-, media-, and print-based worlds as shaping the practices of everyday life. These worlds signify particular ways of thinking and being ... 'Knowing', as we define it here, represents the ways that people think through digital and nondigital environments through their engagement with technologies as they constantly move in and out of print and digital texts.

(Collier and Rowsell, 2020, p 92)

So, this chapter proceeds to look at how online learning in virtual higher education spaces relates to these multiple ways of knowing for and by students; how relational, co-creational partnerships in virtual (digital) spaces allow for the integration of these knowledge repertoires across digital and nondigital practices and the extent to which these virtual spaces are or could be transgressive while still framed by the neoliberal imperatives of universities.

Critical question for practice

» What new 'habitus clash' impediments do we need to address in the virtual domain?

Digital pedagogy frameworks

Principles, practices and framing strategies for virtual higher education need to be placed on a space–time continuum with three points of configuration.

1 The 'old normal', whereby virtual learning was either 'signed up to' as an alternative to campus experience or integrated into learning design together with face to face interaction.

2 The 2020 Covid 'pivot', accepted as essential but hoped to be temporary.

3 The 'new normal' projections of great change in the future as the sector reappraises its modus operandi.

An early example of the latter is the *Learning and Teaching Reimagined* report from Jisc (Maguire et al, 2020). This 'new dawn', drawn out of dialogue with over a thousand UK university participants, identifies a set of key shifts put into play by the pandemic – with 'digital' to be core to university culture; blended learning at the heart of economic modelling; and curriculum design and digital skills enhancement for students and staff to be a priority for the sector. The consensus from the research was that, across staff and students, there is little desire to return to face to face teaching as the default setting.

Students' ideal learning mode is a blended approach using a mixture of pre-recorded, online and live, in-person classes. The flexibility of pre-recorded material is seen as helpful for many students as a way to watch again or watch at a time that suits them. Students say that lectures, whether live or recorded, need to be engaging. In their view online tutorials and seminars need to be in small groups, and lecturers should ensure that they are supportive and encourage students to meet and chat with others. This is especially important for first years who might struggle to meet their peers when participating in online learning and teaching.

(Maguire et al, 2020, p 12)

In addition to those preferences for the organisation of learning, students told the researchers three relational things that seem to align with the principles this book is setting out – that online learning is interconnected with lived *experiences* in complex and personal ways; that the *use* of tech and tools is the operative discerning quality; and that we need to move away from assumptions about not only access to technology and speed of connection but also digital confidence, as this is much more varied among students than we think, as well as being a concern among lecturers, as we know. This debunks, if it wasn't already debunked, the myth of the 'digital native', but it also seems to support the author of that notion, Marc Prensky's, other, and more helpful, contribution (2010), the distinction between nouns (the tools, tech, platforms) and verbs (what we do with them).

Notwithstanding the view that digital 'toolkits' or 'frameworks' are in themselves constraining and out of step with the testimony from students above, which seems to require more organic and open co-design of the virtual space, or at least the situated and social practices therein, how can such texts be mapped to the four relational principles set out for this chapter – *personalised, dialogic, formative and engaging?*

Jisc's *Digital Pedagogy Toolkit* (2020) asks: what makes an *engaging* course on the virtual learning environment? Alongside staff guidance for policy, technology and staff development, a re-evaluation of how we interact with students is recommended for the shift to virtual, suggesting, again, a blend of real time and asynchronous learning, for the reasons by now established, but fleshing this out with a breakdown of factors relating to skills, motivation, knowledge and environment. Learning design advice is 'outsourced' to Gilly Salmon's Carpe Diem and its adaptation by Oxford Brookes and UCL. These ways of working converge expertise and foster interdisciplinary environments, using storyboarding for 'rapid course design'.

The extent to which students experience *engagement* in virtual learning is commonly theorised as 'transactional distance' (Moore, 1993; for application to online education see McBrien, Jones and Cheng, 2009). This theory posits an inter-relation of dialogue, structure and learner autonomy and four modes of interaction: learner–instructor, learner–learner, learner–content and learner–interface interactions. For the experience of distance to be reduced, designers of virtual learning need to maximise the three elements across all of the four interactional contexts. This approach does, however, imply a deficit model of distance, as observed in McBrien et al's (2009, p 13) application and analysis of participants' experiences:

Many of these students may never initiate comments in a traditional classroom. In such cases, the transaction distance enables such students to formulate their ideas and receive responses to them, thus increasing their learning potential.

The question, though, is whether the distance matters, whether we need to worry about reducing the experience of the distance for students or seeing the positives in it, as the findings above suggest.

Critical question for practice

» What are the best practices, in the virtual space, for negotiating the traverse between the 'neoliberal' sector and aspirations for creative 'co-creation' with students as partners? Or, put bluntly, how do we justify asking students to co-design the online product they are paying so much to consume?

On 'zooming out'

This collaborative approach to planning student activity is one of the many examples of pedagogic work that has been foregrounded by the move to the 'all virtual' oxymoron. Mihai (2020) pitches the virtue of this asynchronous learning design in terms of an escape through 'zooming out' from real time (and, indeed, the platform in question) to reconnect with teaching:

Let go of the idea that students are not learning when you don't see them or when you're not around. Instead, challenge yourself to create activities you know will keep them engaged regardless of space and time. Remember who your students are and be creative.
(Mihai, 2020)

The visual representation of a learning sequence is familiar to the arts, humanities and media disciplines; to state the obvious, this is like a visual script for the learning story you want your students to engage with. To continue the zooming metaphor, this is the width of the lens – when we plan our teaching and our students' learning, we have the bigger picture (wide angle) and the micro detail. So, we are thinking about learning 'scenes' that provide a narrative arc towards the learning objectives. The progression from scene to scene is the important bit; does the story make sense in either a more or less linear sequence? Like a Netflix drama, the narrative must be engaging and offer sufficient variety to be so.

Up to this point, there is little here that is so different online. But the storyboarding approach asks us to imagine our virtual space as something our students move through, as a journey, again, like the scenes in a film. Thinking of our students as an audience and considering the story from their perspectives, and moving through the narrative in their own time and at their own pace, rather than in timetabled synchronous attendance. But of fundamental importance is the length of the series, to continue the analogy. This should be the same accumulation of time as planned for, just like a TV drama can be paused and continued later but is still the same duration. Mihai's workshops on storyboarding for virtual learning take participants through modality (asynchronous, blend of individual and collaborative working, independent working with ratios of teacher presence); time-setting for tasks; sequencing; guidance and feedback – like the appearances of characters in a plot – and the 'zoom out' to learning objectives. Returning to the intersection of *relational* learning design with *engagement*, storyboarding also enables us, perhaps more easily, to think deeply about the screen as the conduit, the connecting point or membrane between the institutional frame for learning and lifeworld, but the learning space is way beyond the screen, just as the lecture theatre is only an establishing shot and the seminar room a bridging sequence or piece of dialogue within a much bigger script. A way to open up a dialogue about learning and knowledge is to have students produce their own storyboards, visually and reflexively, 'mapping' their own relational experiences of the curriculum, our interactions, screens, homes, their environments, each other and non-human objects, with 'things'.

Holley (2021) poses critical questions about how we can take a humanising, embodied curriculum into online spaces and asserts the principle of 'clarifying the expectations of the digital', drawing on Nordmann et al's (2020) work on how to build communities online. Holley shares her 'study apron' activity, connected to study journaling, collage work and reflective sketchbooks. These are 'old school' material and intellectual pursuits shared via the affordances of online space (in this case, Padlet – an online board tool allowing for a virtual collage to be constructed by a group). This pivot to creativity for digital learning (Holley's phrasing) thus places the socio-material, digital and nondigital 'post-human' assemblage into humanising objectives (my conceptualisation).

Bennett (2021) emphasises the design thinking inherent to online learning and how this has been more overt than hitherto in the Covid 'pivot', this observation coming after just one month of lockdown learning:

We have witnessed teacher design thinking in 'high speed' mode over the past month. What would it take for us to capitalise on these capabilities and push us towards a learning design revolution? ... In this crisis, a bright light has been shone on the sophisticated work that teachers do. Just as we nurture our students' problem solving skills to prepare them to be innovators in a complex world let's nurture design thinking by our teachers so that their design practices can reshape education for whatever the future brings.

Relational, embodied ... virtual?

This chapter challenges the false binary between 'real' and 'virtual' – the latter depends on the former to signify. 'Third space', from Chapter 1, relies on a distinction between home and campus, albeit with the complication of the 'home from home' first space some students occupy. So, in Covid times, educators are wondering whether, in time, the second space will re-emerge or whether we are *all* in the third space now. If so, then it would cease to have meaning, or at least the 'working from home'/'living at work' debate would frame the categorisation of the hybrid first and second spaces. This is even more pronounced with virtual, as it only makes meaning by its apparently secondary equivalence, to the real. So why a false binary?

This book is about online learning, rather than online learning taking place at the same time as classroom interactions. That situation became much more common during the pandemic in UK schools, where the children of 'key workers' (those deemed to be unable to work from home) were taught in class while everyone else was on screen. However, this 'hybrid' model may be an aspect of the 'new normal', in time, in higher education, and if so, then the false binary is more clearly and presently exposed. Crook and Crook (2020) offer strategies for managing the immediate complexities of doing both at once in this way: simulating in-person experience by 'integrating across modalities'; ensuring breakout rooms have 'clear deliverables' so they feed back coherently to the face to face discussion; using interactive tools such as polling and quizzing; and making sure the online part of the equation is differentiated and positively so, in 'Covid times', the virtual attendees are mask less and thus better placed for some modes of input, it is argued.

Another aspect of the false binary is about the presence and absence of a student. Back now to the fully online, or virtual, experience, what does it mean to be 'there', asks Mihai (2021a), who suggests being present is a combination of intentionality practices, with building connections, communication, clarity of expectations and agility in response to the relative 'presence' of students:

Being present online is not equivalent to unlimited availability. It also does not have to be (all) synchronous. It's the small touches that count the most. Find an approach that suits you and make sure to bring students along, as co-creators of their learning space. You get to decide what kind of presence you will have in the course and that is no easy task ... It's all about finding a balance. Sometimes this means you need to step back. Other times it means you need to step forward.

Recent work on humanising higher education has foregrounded the *relational* practices we are also observing at play in the more engaging virtual spaces for online learning. Devis-Rozental and Clarke (2020) describe these practices as 'embodied', harnessing and investing in a 'relational energy' which is generated through understanding learning as a personal journey and the conception of a sense of place for the journey, or a location for the narrative to return to our storyboard metaphor (my adaptation). This work does not separate out online or virtual engagement or spaces from campus and neither does it view embodiment as physically present. Waight and Holley (2020, and see Holley, 2021, and above) apply the framework to nurse education in digital modes:

Humanising the learning experience for students who are in the learning journey of digital literacy will require important and nuanced skills from the teacher ... Teacher and student interactions based on meaningful connections and non-judgemental interactions provide a safe environment for learning new and different digital skills. The humanizing dimensions of insiderness, uniqueness, agency, togetherness, personal journey, sense of place, sense-making and embodiment and what matters to students is central to achieve this.

(Waight and Holley, in Devis-Rozental and Clarke, 2020, p 138)

In later chapters, critical questions are asked about the idea that online learning *might* provide spaces where the decolonising of curriculum and discipline know-ledge regimes can be activated with less restriction than on campus (as learning's design principles are exposed and negotiated more freely) and about the way that 'futuring' for online learning reproduces Enlightenment discourses about scientific salvation. These are maybe well-intentioned, but risk repeating 'colonial extractivism' (McLean, 2021, p 10) when social justice and decolonial practices are assumed to be an objective for the use of technological platforms which themselves evade cri-tique. The philosophical underpinning of such futuring is at odds with the relational energy this chapter explores, since the relational self exists without the subject/other separation inherent to Western thinking, being in part derived more from Eastern philosophies. Therefore, in addition to the colonial practices we risk re-doing, there is also the seemingly more straightforward problem that mixing relational peda-gogies with technological solutionism by understanding the student experience in terms of the singular student self is unlikely to work:

Much of the rise in populism and nationalism in the West is a backlash against the gradual erosion of belonging. What I find powerful about this way of understanding the problem is that it suggests the deep causes are cultural, a matter of the West becoming too 'Western'. What allowed it to rise is now what is making it weak.

(Baggini, 2018, p 251)

Moving forward into a consideration of examples, the above elements can be integrated with the over-arching practices – relational and dialogic.

MEDIA, COMMUNICATION & COVID-19

THURSDAYS
3:00-4:00PM

join by clicking the
zoom link below

Join our Cloud HD Video....
Zoom is the leader in modern
enterprise video communications,....
bournemouth-ac-uk.zoom.us

zoom
CLICK

8TH OCT — Xin Zhao
The role of social media in political participation during China's COVID-19 pandemic mitigation

15TH OCT — Alexandra Alberda
Data Comics & Graphic Medicine during COVID-19

22ND OCT — Anastasia Kavada
Creating a hyperlocal infrastructure of care: COVID-19 mutual aid groups and digital media

29TH OCT — Liz Maseen Deese
Counter-mapping COVID-19: From maps of crisis to maps of resistance

12TH NOV — Mehita Iqani
Necessity, Surface Statement: The Cultural Politics of Face Masks

19TH NOV — Elinor Carmi
Data Literacies in COVID-19 Times

26TH NOV — Fabian Frenzel, Isabella Rega & the Lockdown Stories Research Collective
Lockdown Stories: Digital Storytelling and Community Empowerment

3RD DEC — Lina Dencik
The Datafied Welfare State: A perspective from the UK

10TH DEC — Julian McDougall
Propaganda vs. Conspiracy: Is Media Literacy Mind over Media?

17TH DEC — Anna Feigenbaum
Policing and Protest during a Pandemic

FEATURED TALK

RACIAL CAPITALISM AND COVID-19

zoom
CLICK

TUESDAY
OCT 27TH

4:00-
5:00PM

DR. WHITNEY PIRTLE

Figure 2.1 MAMC Speaker series.

Example 2.1

Contemporary perspectives 360 #1

This unit was 'pivoted' not only to the virtual space but also to the focus on Covid as the public experience of the pandemic was clearly contemporary in extremis and subject to many mediated perspectives. The unit lead, Anna Feigenbaum, is a well-known scholar in the fields of media, data, public health, protest and activism, and she also runs the postgraduate programme for which this unit, *Contemporary Perspectives in Media and Communication*, contributes a foundational induction.

This unit was 'pivoted' not only to the virtual space but also to the focus on Covid as this subject was clearly so subject to contemporary, mediated perspectives. This put in play a 'postmodern' layering, in the sense that the reflexive learning dimension was about the lived experience of being a student on the unit at university, in the world, during lockdowns. The 'basket of time' was allocated across synchronous guest lectures (see Figure 2.1), preceded by seminars that combined real time seminar discussions with asynchronous but time-specific preparatory work for the lectures. For each of the ten lectures, students signed up for roles – chair, note-taker, pre-talk researcher. OneNote was used to collate and curate the preparatory work; Zoom was used for the lectures and seminars; Padlet was used for collaborative activities in response to pre-recorded or curated open access content. Asynchronous activities included curating memes; uploading examples of propaganda and conspiracy to an interactive educational resource; sharing links to international examples of 'datafied' society; through Padlet; contributing to a Spotify playlist of pandemic related music; and uploading a storyboard. These more active moments of progression towards the learning outcomes served as dynamic 'bridges' between the theoretical reading and note-taking and the guest lectures. One-to-one tutorials were scheduled in the final week prior to the assignment which consisted of three related elements: a text-based blog post (see Figure 2.2) responding to a guest talk for which this role had been assigned; a visual blog (or vlog) about an assigned key concept from the unit; and a 2000-word critical reflection on the competing perspectives around the key concept with regard to Covid.

Media, Communication and COVID-19
A BU MAMC Speaker Series

Getting Through a Pandemic: Mutual Aid and COVID-19

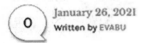
January 26, 2021
Written by EVABU

Never in our lifetimes did we think that we would be living through a global pandemic. We never thought that pubs and clubs would close their doors; let alone shops, schools, parks and country boarders. But they did, and boy is it a tough change. It's a change that has affected people's lives to the point where the elderly can't even step outside without feeling anxious, and the friendly pub owner on the high-street has not been able to open his doors for months, but still has to pay rent. It is one where the public have felt somewhat abandoned by the

Figure 2.2 Eva's blog.

In Example 2.1, the unit as a whole purposely blended academic learning with digital literacies, perhaps a less challenging combination for a media unit at M level than for other disciplines, so that the requirements for assessment included references to assigned reading from the guest talks and to independently sourced peer-reviewed research on the key concept aligned with hyperlinks, tags, visualisation, videos or webcomics. Across all aspects, the stated criteria mapped across critical reading, reflection on lived experience and relational dialogue with others to compare perspectives and digital curation of the topic under scrutiny. The approach taken to the storyboarding of the unit for virtual engagement with a 'basket of time' over virtual seminars, guest speaker masterclasses and asynchronous activity can be *described* by being broken down into the core elements – *tools, resources* and the *learning narrative* – *assessed* for its facilitation of *personalised, dialogic, formative* and *engaging* virtual education and *discussed* with regard to students' reflections on the sense of place, insiderness, the duality of personalised agency and feeling of being together and the development of *new* digital skills. The importance of this 'case study' hinges on the unit leader's vision in using the virtual imposition to harness resources that could not be utilised in physical space, so the unit's asynchronous activities and real-time seminars all related to a series of guest talks and 'masterclasses' by external, guest academics who would not have travelled to a lecture theatre on the south coast of England during the winter and would also have been less likely to contribute to a hybrid model with them on a 'big screen' and students on campus. This intervention raises an important question for the future about the extension of networks and how we might all disseminate our work to students, via such inputs, so our research informs curriculum more directly, eroding institutional gatekeeping as well as breaching space and time.

It could be argued that the cohort for this unit was easy to 'pivot' if we think about the configuration of discipline, level and context. As stated, the present tense theorisation of the immediate experience reduced the sense of virtual distance; the postgraduate expectations are different for 'contact time'; and the international cohort provided a richer blend of contrasting examples and opportunities to enrich the collaborative learning through space and time flexibility, with the virtual space reducing some of the unintended inequalities at work on campus, perhaps. It is, therefore, important to compare this example with another example from the far end of the space–time continuum.

Space–time continuum

The critical questions posed here about relational practices, how we use tools and resources and how we storyboard learning as a narrative might tend to be more enthusiastically answered by disciplines at the far end of the continuum where the 'virtual' is less so, as can be speculated with regard to the postgraduate media unit above. Those are the subjects where the online 'version' of lectures, seminars and enquiry-based learning might be a matter of preference or opportunity.

In the case of Dance, Rob Kitsos of Simon Fraser University in Canada suggests that teaching online has improved the personalised learning experience for students and their confidence in interaction:

Aspects of online teaching I see as advantages — like each student being able to have their own focus without the competition or distraction of other people in the room or mirrors. We also seem to have more conversations as students seem to feel more open to speaking on Zoom than in the studio.

(Kitsos, 2020)

But, again, this is about the short-term imposition of the virtual and not a permanent shift. How could that work?

Frances Clarke is Dean of Dance at Trinity Laban Conservatoire of Music and Dance. She was interviewed for this book and was firstly asked, thinking beyond Covid into the long term, simply can a Dance degree be studied online?

Not entirely, but blended, yes. Fully online would be detrimental as in a conservatoire environment, students need the studio experience. The nature of practice, skills and technique, tactile feedback and spaces, sites for learning, are key. Coaching and performance enhancement, supplementary training can be online, and can add value. But the physical face to face relationship is needed for motivation, self-discipline and self-efficacy.

Moving on from space to time, is the asynchronous dimension an opportunity or must a Dance cohort be together in 'real time'?

We do need to be together in real time, yes. During lockdown, even, with a blended model, we have been running reduced size, real time studio classes. It is absolutely essential, because the level is so physically and psychologically challenging, it has to be face to face feedback, that's particularly pertinent for rehearsals, where you have to be together. But we have had great success with asynchronous classes too, and students have loved it, so for us it's the combination that is needed. Students have reported being more focused, concentrating better when they can access things in their own time, and that's also given them a greater sense of autonomy.

Zooming in on autonomy and linking this to inclusion and access:

There are several different factors, it's not just that they are online but that in smaller groups, they can feel more confident to engage, but due to being online, they feel less 'watched', that constant surveillance is a real issue in Dance training which comes from a tradition of quite autocratic teaching and the body is viewed intensively. I will argue that we don't teach that way at Trinity Laban, but nevertheless that feeling of being further removed and even if you teach in a strong, motivational environment, the nature of Dance is moving in front of others in big spaces, and that is hard to cope with at times, so there has been some benefit of working in your own space, turning off cameras, when appropriate, or moving out of the space or changing the angle, that choice of how you are seen has been interesting and something we need to investigate more. But that is part of the training, so the dilemma is that whilst we'll have a stronger blended approach, students will still be predominately with us in the building, so that distancing can only be partial, for feedback, from tutors but also from peers, teamwork and related-ness, they underpin the motivational framework for us.

The perennial tension in the blend is clearly articulated here, the clarity in the position that the curriculum can yield so far to a greater autonomy and set of choices for how to see and be seen, in this case. But in the case of Dance, Clarke is clear that creative practices are inextricably linked to experiences of visibility and embodiment from which the online elements can only offer a temporary evasion. Leeds University's *Physical Theatre Online* (Digital Education Leeds, 2020) initiative might appear to offer an alternative view, but students engaging with 'Exploring the Slap' work through a series of online resources and then produce a written response, design a storyboard and record a performance, but these are individual activities followed by self-evaluation and peer assessment; therefore, while this does achieve embodied community learning in a virtual space, clearly 'moving in front of others in big spaces' is harder to replicate.

While this is the case in all disciplines, as the English Literature student, on a blended programme, will be expected to share her thoughts in a seminar room with no 'camera off' option, it seems that for Dance there is a discipline of another kind, a rigorous exposure that is part of the learning as opposed to an aspect of its social context.

Performative pedagogy (Campbell, 2020) is a reflexive process for integrating art, design and performance into teaching through disruptions, including *technoparticipation*. In an open studio, 'live listening in March 2021', Campbell discussed these approaches with Pauline de Souza and Mark Childs with two focal points that add to this consideration of distance – possibilities for enabling intimacy in the virtual space and 'embracing the glitch'.

The former is about making changes to screen layouts to ensure that we are all experiencing a shared virtual space rather than our individual spaces linked by a platform, but also through the embodying possibilities of virtual reality, using avatars, sharing a virtual reality space for a meeting, enabling gestures to appear on the screen. The latter is about allowing glitches, frozen screens and other interruptions to be part of the life of online learning, just as a 'real world' gathering will include interruptions, but embracing these as 'creative interruptions' that can generate intimacy on another level, as playful fallibility. Going further, *Touch my Touch* (Lancel and Maat, 2021) is an experiment that has been cited for its potential to inform online education. Facial biometric monitoring was used to enable touch to be experienced in virtual spaces, to reclaim the space of artificial intelligence:

Current technological research into touch often focusses on bio-metric control and surveillance technologies, AI algorithms, profiling and/or social media which often raise questions about our privacy and shared agency online. Touch My Touch in contrast presents touching as a playful, explorative experience, encouraging people to engage with necessary new forms of online connection; exploring and shaping future narratives of touch, through touch.

Critical question for practice

» Where can our specific, situated pedagogy be on the space–time continuum in relation to the examples described above – the virtual Dance studio standing in for what is needed, the postgraduate media unit which deconstructs its own conditions of possibility embracing the glitch and virtual touch? The same question applies to the following examples – radical claims made for disruptive, open learning, Teach Outs and the Teach In?

Teach Outs

Teach Outs are a feature of university industrial action. They are free, public events that take place during strikes, usually outside campuses, organised by pickets. As such, they share characteristics with open learning, but with a very different relationship to the institution they Teach Out from, at least by first appearances. In March 2020, the University and College Union (UCL) ran a workshop on Greening Film Education, consisting of a Teach Out on environmentalism followed by a workshop on film-making using portable media. Teach Outs during the strike tended to be 'third spaces' between public academic work – bringing the content of higher education outside, physically outside the campus but also outside of the usual boundaries around disciplines and registrations – and the socio-political campaign themes around the action, in this case the environmental sustainability of the workshop is part of a broader concern with the political economy of higher education, precarious labour and the marketisation of academia. Tablets were taken out of the university to the picket line, where they were used by participants in response to the 'Teach Out' by an environmental film-maker, and the results were uploaded to YouTube. A member of staff who was not able to attend due to access constraints was represented by a robot avatar.

But can a Teach Out take place in a virtual space and are its rules of engagement dependent on an overt, activism that, if not directed as a resistance to the university itself, is by necessity happening 'out' because of a need to be in an outsider in relation to aspects of the system, conditions or practices that are inside the building? When 'we are the campus', what is the outside in this relation?

The University of Michigan provides 'Teach Outs' in the form of free and open online learning events. These events feature presentations from university academics and discussions among participants, with the call for those connecting to 'consider actions you can take in your own community.' This approach is a combination of aspects of MOOCs and smaller-scale open learning provision (see below) with the kinds of civic agency associated with physical Teach Outs, such as those organised by unions, as above. The objectives are discussion and sharing perspectives, as opposed to consuming content for the development of skills or the acquisition of knowledge. Topics covered recently, at the time of writing, include fake news and disinformation; discussing politics and debates; LGBTQ pride; police brutality; 'Civil Rights in the Trump Era'; free speech on campus; augmented reality; and practising gratitude. Teach Outs last for either two weeks or four; they are designed as 'just in time community learning events'. Compared to the UCU Teach Outs, the shared dynamics are the emphasis on university academics in a 'third space' exchange with participants and the left-leaning concerns with matters of democracy and equality (among some more 'instrumental' courses). The difference is that this is teaching out in a virtual space but from within the university, with a mutual endorsement therein; the 'out' is therefore not against, or 'away from', politically.

A 'Teach In' might sound like the opposite, but that would be to be complicit in another false binary. In December 2020, teachers and lecturers were invited to a free, online event in five languages on sustainable development framed by the United Nations Sustainable Development Goals:

Participation is made easy: Simply create and/or 'adopt' a sustainable development presentation of your choice and include this in your teaching lessons on 4 December 2020! You can share your teaching experience with us on social media and via discussion boards, and network with fellow learners around the world on the platform.

(Haw Hamburg, 2020)

In this case, the theme comes 'in' from a global network, and then the learning and teaching activity within the classroom flows back 'out'. The objective is shared perspective and pedagogic knowledge transfer enabled by the digital environment and open access network. The 'third space' is the network, the membrane between the external or over-arching theme and the pedagogic adaptation and practices of participants, so we can think about the first space as the classroom and the second space as the UN, even, which would be a relational conversion, as the first space here is hitherto the second. Fiona Cownie, Associate Professor in Relational Approaches to Higher Education, participated in the Teach In and reflects:

The teach in format felt participatory and accessible; the event gave me a better understanding of how to integrate open access material into my teaching. The live sessions were drawn from academics across the globe; those I attended embraced one from my own University to an institution in Canada. There was a real global feel to the event and an energy behind the sustainability agenda.

Critical question for practice

» How can the online or virtual dimension emancipate you from institutional boundaries and how is this sustainable longer-term, beyond the novelty of the 'rapid response' to lockdowns or 'at home if you can' culture?

Open education

The open education movement has been asking critical questions about online for a long time, critical questions about the role of the university itself in the digital age. It goes without saying that Covid brought such debates to the surface with clear and present urgency, but the focus here is on the more foundational and long-standing lines of enquiry. 'Open learning' can range from an institutional strategy within a more conventional structure (eg, at Coventry University rather than at the Open University). In this case, the development and provision of open educational resources, as opposed to only those enrolled on, and paying for, courses, are a tactical deployment of mobile technologies in education to create transgressive learning communities and challenge the classroom boundary to reach the people outside the institution in new learning 'audience communities' and foster creative practitioner networks. At Coventry, moving out from the Disruptive Media Learning Lab, open programmes are freely available and link participants to a number of networks and communities of specialists, practitioners and mentors, but this open activity is connected synchronously with the classroom:

In our own particular hybrid take on 'blended learning', classes on these courses are open online to anyone, anywhere, to participate in, add to the discussions and even rip remix and mash-up. This applies to the schedule, lectures, lesson content, exercises and assignments, recommended reading, recorded talks and interviews with visiting speakers (audio and video), RSS feeds, tag clouds and blog post archive, as well as a number of practical 'how to' videos, all of which are available under a CC-BY-SA license. The use of blogs and social media platforms means that participants – both the in class ('atoms-based'), accredited, fee paying participants and those taking these classes for free remotely – can interact and contribute through discussion, feedback, suggestions etc. In this way the syllabus becomes a 'co-authored script', curated by the academic team but produced by the collective exchange and effort of the learning community.

(Van Mourik Broekman et al, 2014, p 99)

This long quote is necessary because of the important constituent elements, which cover the hybrid pedagogy model, the enabled opportunities for agentive engage-ment ('remix', for example), licensing protocols and fees. But equally important is the date, given the source quoted is a summary of ongoing activity; this is from nearly a decade ago at the time of writing.

The Disruptive Media Learning Lab locates open education in a complex environ-ment, regarding which *'one effective way to understand HEIs is as sites of contest-ation between divergent constituencies whose needs are often incommensurate and operating on disparate timescales'* (Van Mourik Broekman et al, 2014, p x). The threat posed to the order of things in higher education by MOOCs might not have come to pass but the open movement can still be understood as partly a response *to* the threat and partly a harnessing of the potential for productive disruption that the conditions of possibility for MOOCs generated. 'Connectivism and Connective Knowledge' was the first MOOC on record, in 2008. This offered a hybrid model, fee payers working with open access cohorts. In the decade that followed, one genre of MOOC fostered a digital realisation of constructivist learning principles while another genre provided a 'transmission repository' with some conventional interactive aspects. Within both genres, MOOCs were usually provided by well-financed institutions as partly a recruitment strategy (especially with an eye on international students) for their campus offer:

MOOCs do have the potential to be disruptive, but generally it is only elite institutions that are financially viable who can consider offering them in the first place, as they are generally expensive to run, especially if conducted in pedagogically sound ways.

(Ng'ambi and Bozalek, 2015, p 452)

Returning to the need to deconstruct and challenge 'false binaries', open learning as far as those that consider it a movement are concerned is more of an 'either–and' than an 'either–or'. Shaun Hides, from the Coventry project, reflects here on the sense of working out (open) but from within (the university):

So, to ask what might the future of a University be, what might we want to hold onto out of that space and what kinds of experiments might we want to do, is to try to offer a different course through that globalised, neo-colonial version of higher education that is striving to make every bit of educational content into something easily consumable from wherever and however. So, to hold onto some of those attributes, values, approaches and critical engagements that disciplines have entailed, but it's got to be reconfigured into a new constellation, a new mode of operation.

On the student experience, at the point of being explicit about this way of working, from course to department level, every single metric has increased for the better. Numbers have increased, engagement with what we are judged and valued on has increased. So, the evidence suggests that for us, it's the right way of working.

(McDougall, 2015, p 6)

The false binaries Hides resists here are those between the neoliberal university and the progressive mode of operation exemplified by open learning and between the boundary-crossing and potentially risky opening out of such pedagogic practices with internal performance indicators.

However, while we can trace back this self-testimony to Coventry University's 'performance' and rankings and take such triangulation as sufficient to make Hides a credible witness, that was then and much more recently evidence has been presented to the contrary, with regard to student satisfaction with the online experience. An Australian Government review (Martin, 2020) scanned 118 higher education providers and produced findings that suggest a mixed but often negative experience, for students, of engagement with tutors and interaction with peers, both of which were significantly reduced in the move to online learning during Covid. On further scrutiny, these negative feelings were often related to the comparison with 'before', the campus experience, and often starkly socio-material, for example, lower interaction due to students feeling awkward about having the camera on while at home with family members present, a kind of complex habitus hybridity we might conclude. Where students have various coping options for the habitus clash they experience when moving to university from 'non-traditional' routes, whether successful or not, this is much harder to negotiate when you are at university and at home simultaneously, perhaps. But this is not to underplay the students' responses; they were clearly negative and we cannot have it both ways: the sector cannot claim a paradigm shift to blended learning, post-Covid, if the evidence for such is not consistent. It is more a contextual point about the need for the online learning experience to be 'the space', as opposed to a version of something else, as outlined in Chapter 1; the importance of a 'we are the campus' mindset, and for students to have signed up for it, instead of being on screen and locked down. And the logical conclusion of this is that the best virtual learning *isn't* virtual as that idea takes us back to the 'real thing' that we are not doing. It's just learning.

And as well as being 'just learning', it is also material. The false binary is not only about real on campus at one end and virtual at home at the other; there is also an opposition of physical and virtual that doesn't hold when scrutinised to any degree. To put it simply, it's not just 'the screen' but the screen and the person in another place. Not on campus, but still a place, so the campus is a lot of different places, now, but not 'no place'. When the illusion of screen neutrality is interrupted by a parcel delivery, pet intrusion or 'homeschooling fail', we shouldn't see this as the exception to some notion of a disembodied, impersonal norm. This 'topological multiplicity' gets us out of the 'either–or' illusion, but it raises more critical 'either and both' questions, as '*the university is seen to be "enacted" at a distance via various conceptions of spatiality, as opposed to falling on one side or other of a simplistic "static" versus "mobile" binary*' (Gourlay, 2021, p 6).

Summary

This chapter has been about:

- the potential for virtual learning to be 'the best it can be' by rendering itself obsolete, in a good way;

- in other words, virtual learning is not about being a version of something else, a substitute or supplement, but in a post-human, socio-material 'fusion' of tools, tech and people, to become more human than the on-campus experience;

- we are, then, moving towards seeing distance as a positive, as more dialogic and profoundly relational. This requires a leap of faith.

Useful texts

Devis-Rozental, C and Clarke, S (2020) *Humanising Higher Education: A Positive Approach to Enhancing Wellbeing*. Basingstoke: Palgrave MacMillan.

Foregrounds the concept of relational energy and the responsibility for higher education institutions to humanise the student journey. As such this is an important framing for a critique of online learning's relational post-humanism. In addition to the over-arching relevance, one chapter explores in detail the nurturing of digital competence for well-being.

Disruptive Media Learning Lab: https://dmll.org.uk/

The DMLL at Coventry University is a physical space but also a hub for innovative open learning, as described in the quotes above. On this site, the visitor can sample tools and strategies and read about the pedagogic principles.

Hawley et al (2019) Students as Partners in Third Spaces. *International Journal of Students as Partners.* [online] Available at: https://doi.org/10.15173/ijsap. v3i1.3980 (accessed 2 June 2021).

Special issue devoted to the third space partnerships which curate a collection of research outputs to argue that students' and teachers' ways of being in third spaces, as well as the pedagogies required by them, are qualitatively different to orthodox teaching spaces because they demand that the values and cultural capital of participants be an explicit element of the learning. This collection links the theoretical principles set out in Chapter 1 with the focus in this chapter on relational practices.

Nørgård, R T (2020) *Meet the Education Researcher – Interview with Neil Selwyn,* November 2020. [online] Available at: https://soundcloud.com/ eetheducationesearcher/design-and-the-ethics-of-higher-education-rikke-toft-norgard (accessed 2 June 2021).

This is a great introduction to pioneering projects on design and ethics in higher educa-tion. These are not exclusive to the online space, far from it, but the 'University of We' and 'Playful University' projects discussed here offer insights into the role of design thinking in ethical online university practices.

University of Michigan Teach Outs: https://online.umich.edu/teach-outs/

As discussed in this chapter, these Teach Outs are about more than just promoting the university and its courses but extend out to a set of social justice objectives. The Teach Outs available here are part of a broader project of engendering a 'learning lifestyle' for problem-solving, equity and inclusivity, access and affordability 'at scale'. This is an example of online learning 'out of' higher education for a different, more ambitious purpose.

This chapter reviews the notion of 'constructive alignment' of feedback to learning and digital contexts.

Critical questions for practice

» How do, can and could transformative third space digital practices translate into assessment?

» Where can you see a critical, dynamic and inclusive alignment of porous expertise, relational co-creation, student partnership and social justice peda-gogy with assessment design in the virtual university?

If we wish to discover the truth about an educational system, we must look into its assessment procedures. What student qualities and achievements are valued and rewarded by the system? How are its purposes and intentions realised? To what extents are the hopes and ideals, aims and objectives professed by the system ever truly perceived, valued and striven for by those who make their way within it? The spirit and style of student assessment defines the de facto curriculum.

(Rowntree, 1977, p 9)

If pedagogic relations are 'up for grabs' in online spaces, as the design of learning is arguably more deconstructive and educators are more likely to 'show the working', either able to or obliged to look awry from the conventions of campus teaching spaces, then the next critical question to ask relates to how that shift in relations is represented in the assessment of students. Jacques Rancière (1991) and Paolo Freire were both sceptical about emancipatory discourses incorporated into conventional learning and teaching hierarchies. Freire cites a letter from workers in Sao Paulo, sceptical about the worthy intentions of '*the ones that come looking for us to teach us that we're oppressed and exploited and to tell us what to do*' (1970, p 63). For this cri-tique, the concern will be around the danger of transformative, relational energy in dynamic learning design being reined in by static assessment design.

For Rancière, the pedagogic relation itself is that which, in Foucauldian terms, exercises power in the unequal expression of expertise. Through this (critical) way of seeing, student engagement and partnership might be simulacra and thus *all the more* oppressive, through the co-option of those we claim to 'liberate' into the idioms of our language games. Ridley (2016) sees the 'flipped classroom' in this way, replicating Rancière's 'division of the sensible' in a reproduction of epistemological hierarchy, not really a disruption, but just the same arrangement 'from home'.

For a decade now, the UK higher education sector has placed a high value on 'students as partners' and this has often been at the heart of 'digital literacy' activities aiming to facilitate collaboration between the students and lecturers towards the co-production of knowledge (see Trowler and Trowler, 2010; Weller and Kandiko Howson, 2014; Bovill, 2020). The Higher Education Academy (HEA), now Advance HE, presented a set of 'new pedagogical ideas' in 2014: learner empowerment, future-facing education, decolonising education, transformative capabilities, crossing boundaries and social learning, all of which included the harnessing of digital technologies. In previous work (Potter and McDougall, 2016) the enduring political tensions expressed by Freire and Rancière, aforementioned, and also Raymond Williams and Stuart Hall from the Birmingham School of Cultural Studies were found to be at work in the co-creation interventions, either funded by or disseminated by the HEA as the 'new ideas'. Those with more explicit political intentions situated co-creation as a 'shape-shifting', renegotiation of expertise, a form of redistribution through the mobilisation of a 'counterscript' (from Guttierez' conception of third space), markedly distinct from projects at the service of more seemingly neutral objectives for student experience, employability or more recently 'resilience'. Sanders (2020) has warned against the conflation of more complex online learning capabilities with resilience as a threat to critical approaches:

'We don't want you to be critical' – This particular point comes out the back of my own research work on digital technology, which has shifted into a broader educational concern regarding the political configuration of individual resilience *within education. Where digital literacy and notions of critical empowerment that can be associated to addressing this are discursively marginalised for future action, in favour of building* resilience*. The more generalised concern for education directly relates to this – are we at risk of further hollowing out of more general critical literacies development within education, if political policy and industry-based generic solutions for addressing individual* resilience *become pervasive?*

(Sanders, 2020)

The discursive intersect

The way we think and talk about and practise assessment is complicated but it usually relates to a discourse of standards that 'always-already' depends on other discourses – of performativity, accountability and surveillance. These overlap but, crucially, 'standards' in and of themselves are an 'empty signifier' which we can't really be opposed to, but at the same time are meaningless without recourse to another discourse.

The performativity discourse is in a necessary relationship with thresholds and targets, from the accountability discourse. This discourse audits and displays performance, applying metrics and, increasingly, speaking the inherently biased extractions from data and algorithms. Accountability requires the discourse of surveillance for management and legitimation, through the technologies of those metrics, but also processes of external scrutiny, peer review, benchmarks and league table rankings. The discourse of standards holds these three interconnected discourse 'cells' together, while also being reliant on them. It is both empty and full. Empty in that it can only live through a proximal relation with the other discourses, but also full in that it provides the logic for the other three cells (see McDougall et al, 2006).

Foucault's influence on the sociology of education (see Ball, 1990) sees assessment above all to disseminate the social appropriation of discourse, through the seemingly neutral reproduction of epistemology. Learners in an educational system come to understand about themselves and their relationship with knowledge according to particular assessment discourses, not as an end point 'after epistemology', but, rather above all else. Assessment of any kind, according to Foucault, reveals the truth about subjects to themselves.

Vygotsky's emphasis on reflexive learning and the dilemmas of assessment are influential in constructivist approaches to learning in higher education but assessment is the 'poor relation' in the sense that the pedagogic work influenced by Vygotsky might posit no assessment, or only formative feedback, as the logical conclusion. For example, Campione's (1989) taxonomy of approaches for assisted learning draws on Vygotsky to neatly describe what most assessment *doesn't* measure. Vygotsky's 'zone of proximal development' represents the space between a student's level at a fixed point in time, which can apparently be measured, and her potential development under guidance which is always in motion, moving forward to more of what is being learned, or manifested in practice:

[t]hose functions that have not yet matured but are in the process of maturation, functions that will mature tomorrow but are in the embryonic stage. These functions

41

could be called the 'buds' or 'flowers' rather than the fruits of development. The actual developmental level characterises mental development retrospectively while the zone of proximal development characterises mental development prospectively.

(Vygotsky, 1978, pp 86–7)

The zone of interest to Vygotsky is in between the static point of summative assessment and the future generated by the formative feedback loop, requiring a more dynamic assessment. If learning happens *prospectively*, then it is not only the case that summative assessment is static and fails to measure development in motion, but more starkly, it is also inaccurate and thus fails to be fit for its purpose:

Particularly liable to be misclassified are students who have not had the opportunity to acquire the skills and knowledge assessed on standard tests. In addition, without any way of articulating the processes that may have operated, or failed to operate, to produce a given level of performance, it is not possible to determine how to devise an intervention to improve that performance.

(Campione, in Daniels, 1996, p 226)

The implication of this is that assessment is formulated in higher education to measure standards and levels based on the illusion of a 'level playing field' which is debunked by the same sector's access, participation and EDI (equality, diversity and inclusion) policies. Therefore, no good intentions for social justice and inclusion in higher education can work without close attention to how students are assessed.

Critical question for practice

» What opportunities for this necessary close attention are afforded by online learning?

Hamilton et al here reflect on the way that the constraining imperatives of education are potentially disrupted through online learning:

[c]hallenges an underlying assumption that learning can only be successful or take place in sanctioned, controlled spaces. The participatory nature of the internet has

rendered this idea obsolete, and yet governing institutions persist in ignoring these changes rather than rethinking what teaching and learning is and can be.

(Hamilton et al, 2015, p 216)

However, it is fair to now give credit to universities for awakening to the latter part of this.

When online learning spaces are designed with the intention, as many now are, of transgressing disciplines, power relations and colonial epistemologies, such spaces can be 'saturated' with rich, reciprocal practices, and educational structures can 'shape-shift' to challenge epistemological power relations. Despite the focus necessarily shifting to decolonising and reparation in terms of what knowledge 'is', the kinds of pedagogical renegotiations at work in these digital contexts are often 'old-school' constructivist principles. For Rancière, exemplified in his story about 'ignorant schoolmaster', the stuff of critical pedagogy is a process, never content and experienced and never explained. We would expect digital technology to provide the kinds of third spaces, then, where we can *'reject the need for explication in favour of a community of learning between students that, on the one hand, depends on solidarity between students and, on the other, encourages students to make up their own minds about the material they are given'* (Ridley, 2016, p 9). When online learning starts out from a critical pedagogy starting point, a desire to change the pedagogic relation can be privileged above the neoliberal obligation to commodify the 'learning experience'. It's unlikely that any educational encounter in the kinds of digitally mediated third spaces that start out from a radical pedagogy stance – towards 'democratic indiscipline' – would fail to bring to the surface questions of entitlements, rights, ethics and voice in 'everyday' pedagogy on the part of all the social actors involved.

And yet, how to approach the conservative assessment modalities to which students are obliged to return?

Critical question for practice

» How can you traverse the spaces between 'authentic assessment' in online learning and online proctoring to think more imaginatively about constructive alignment, assessment and trust?

Critical issues

Proctor or authenticate?

The question of how to assess from a distance in online environments often transfers the more static, summative functions of assessment into the virtual space. When that is the intention, the debate over authentic assessment versus 'online proctoring' starts out from the same place as the relative merits of coursework versus exams for the objectives of testing knowledge and skills either through recall or application. Proctoring software has been more enthusiastically adopted in the US than in the UK, where there appears to be more anxiety over the surveillance of students' eye movements and keystrokes and the blocking of their web browsers during the testing period. There are discipline fault lines at play, as in many cases academics from arts, humanities and social sciences already favoured authentic assessment whereas STEM communities have a harder time moving away from exams and are thus less averse to algorithmic invigilation, with the ethics around this moving into a more reflective modality:

Some companies say they have recognised the issue. Keith Straughan, chief executive of Axiologs and one of the developers of UK-based online testing platform Tenjin, said they took these 'concerns very seriously indeed'. Tenjin does not 'take control' of a candidate's computer or use continuous video monitoring; instead it takes frequent photos, biometrically matched against identity documents, and supplements this with voice recognition, he said.

(McKie, 2021)

The narrative of an apparent decline in students' honesty is, of course, in the vested interests of the ed-tech industry. While the reassurances from Tenjin above suggest the insertion of some values into the system, there are more far-reaching problems:

If I take a test using an algorithmic test proctor, it encodes my body as either normal or suspicious and my behaviours as safe or threatening. As a cisgender, able bodied, neurotypical, white man, these technologies generally categorise my body as normal and safe, and because of this, they would not endanger my education, well-being, employment or academic standing. The majority of students on my campus don't share my identities and could have a very different experience being read by test proctoring algorithms. We need to understand the potential ways that algorithmic test proctoring can discriminate against students based on their bodies and behaviours, why higher education is willing to endanger students in the first place, and what we can do about it.

(Swauger, 2020, p 50)

This acceptance of harm is alarming, rooted in hesitation to move on and therein a failure to understand that if we are serious about anti-racist and social justice objectives for online learning in higher education, the eradication of normative bias must be a first principle rather than an afterword to surveillance and standardisation, within the discursive intersect discussed earlier, whereby 'the standard' is always referential to another discourse.

The way that this enduring, static relationship between the two assessment modes for summative testing 'after the event' and the very slow progress towards more dynamic, 'Vygotskian' ways of presenting learning for audiences resonates with the zeitgeist critique of Adam Curtis' *Can't Get You Out of My Head* (2021). Amidst the complex, intertextual ideas at work in the documentary is the dynamic inner mind being at odds with the static, undeveloping civic and political structures. Following this line of thinking, we can see how the slow response of education to the digitally mediated lived experiences of students is also the case in politics, where the choices for the future are not very different from the systems of the past – increasing the state control through surveillance or a 'benign' neoliberalist middle ground, with promises to change the world for better or worse (Obama's 'Yes We Can' and the Occupy movement or Trump and Brexit) failing to do so not because of a lack of political consensus but rather due to a lack of imagination, a space currently filled by polarised discourse and conspiracy, Curtis suggests. A leap it may seem, but there is something in all this about the way that we delimit our imaginations to units of assessment that either test or apply, even when we have the affordances of the web to work with.

Datafication

The use of learner analytics at a senior leadership systems level is increasingly fed down the chain to lecturers, who are encouraged to use small-scale data analytics to monitor students' progress and engagement. The benefit of such 'DIY Learning Analytics' (Lawrence, 2021) is that they can 'trigger' disengagement and aid retention through present-tense monitoring of students' experience, as opposed to the annual review cycle when 'the horse has bolted'.

The concept of the 'hidden curriculum' will be familiar to readers of books in this series, but the need for students to survive the 'habitus clash' of higher education can now be seen to extend to the necessity of data literacy. On the flip side of the value of 'DIY analytics' for lecturers, the datafication of the learning experience and also of students as their digital practices are interconnected to data in the form of learner analytics as a new category of assessment. Ignoring, at best, or deliberately obscuring the power bias in analytics is a form of 'strategic ignorance' (McGoey, 2019), a deliberate data illiteracy, as Mertala argues:

Concerning data (il)literacy, presenting and treating data as undisputed cognitive authority may lead students to overestimate the accuracy of data and to build excessive trust in the reliability of analyses and reports produced by devices and software.

(Mertala, 2020, p 35)

Williamson (2016) has troubled the visualisation of data in education by deconstructing its design variables that serve to reproduce as an objective set of correlations and representations in linear sequences and geometric patterns. Following from this, and Mertala's intervention, it appears that, in keeping with the pursuit of an agentive, dynamic data literacy, this must involve new ways of working with data in addition to a more critical reading of it.

Critical question for practice

» How can higher education academics and students 'do data differently' to expose the 'hidden curriculum' of unstable, partial and inherently biased data in order to tell other stories with the data?

Example 3.1

Doing data differently

This British Academy funded project took place in schools, but has transferable findings for higher education. The research enabled teachers to engage with different, more professionally validating uses of data through visualisations so that socio-material complexity could emerge in resistance to more instrumental presentations of data in education:

> *Our project approached this not through taking a critical stance on existing data practices, but by exploring the kinds of possibilities that might be produced – and connections that might be made – by generating new ones. Working with 'small', 'slow' data in ways that foreground instability, as happened through this project, may create space for acknowledging professional practice as complex, contingent and dependent upon the human, material, relational dimensions of what happens in schools.*
>
> (Burnett et al, 2021, p 124)

Another project which offers, from another place, learnings for higher education in the domain of data literacy, as the critical assessment of data, is *COVID-19: Data Literacy is for Everyone* (Alberda, 2020), for which a webcomic was generated to help empower audiences to better understand the Covid-19 data visualisations that were dominating everyday life. It is not controversial to accept that *'an important element of data visualisation literacy is understanding how different visual representations of the same data can change the story being told and its emotional effects on readers'* (Alberda, 2020). It is not a great leap to argue that students should have opportunities to read the data analytics about their learning and 'engagement' more critically and also to trouble the data by repurposing it to tell other stories.

Critical question for practice

» How can the craft of online assessment design ensure the right balance between innovation and feedback literacy for students?

Crafting feedback for agency

Feedback can prove to be more effective when provided using various media. The multimodality also allows for increased accessibility (eg for students with a disability, students with dyslexia). whether you teach online, face-to-face or in a blended manner, you can use technology tools to diversify the type of feedback you offer – from the more traditional comments in written form, to integrating audio/video feedback or using screencasting for precise and quick feedback.

(Mihai, 2021b)

David Carless' work on assessment in higher education has been consistently influential, so it is to him that the sector can justifiably turn for research-informed insight on how 'assessment for digital futures' (Carless, 2020, 2021) can be designed as learner-oriented to foster 'feedback literacy' in online contexts. The examples he draws from YouTube curation, video presentations, meme-related, assessed blogs and vlog (as exemplified earlier) are mirrored by modes of feedback that utilise audio, video and social media (see Mahoney et al, 2019; Liu, 2018; Hung, 2016). The feedback literacy developed and, arguably, enhanced online is generated by a process of appreciating feedback, making judgements, managing affect and taking action. At the feedback stage, using digital media in online spaces enables rapport, nuance and efficiency, using such tools as voice recognition (see also Jisc, 2016). However, that sense of time saved might not be experienced equally, and Carless warns of innovative assessment feeling like harder work for students if the design fails to link feedback to an agency (see also Nieminen et al, 2021).

Arnold's (2017) study with lecturers using technology for feedback found them working with a highly situated mesh of:

[u]nderlying beliefs, personal biography, academic identity, and recent experience of family members, collegial networks, and quality management systems. Together these components form an operational feedback ecosystem in which the lecturer mediates the complexity and aligns their choices about feedback with their beliefs and values. The creation of feedback through technology appears to be a work of craft.

Crisp (2020) offers a set of research-informed design principles for online assessment, including the scheduling of key, intensive time frames for formative video feedback linked to adaptive learning technology and a strategy to 'make thinking visible' through media. Crucially, Crisp advocates a shift back for learning analytics to a focus on the role of feedback in the quality of learning and to differentiate experiences for bias:

Step into the shoes of a policy maker, philanthropist, grant maker, or an accreditor for a moment. All of them need methods to compare one online learning program with another for the purpose of granting funds or shaping policy that protects students from bad actors in the marketplace. What if the definition of a learner's feedback experience was so widely accepted that any entity could ask of an online learning provider, 'Could you provide data around your learners' feedback experiences for each degree level and program? Could you also provide these data disaggregated by race/ethnicity, gender, and first-generation categorizations?'

(Crisp, 2020)

Critical question for practice

» As assessment formats such as video essays become more common across the curriculum, can they play a role in disrupting the logocentric practices of the academy for a more inclusive future?

Example 3.2

Video essay for sustainable assessment (MPE)

Video essay production has developed as an assessment mode, extending out from media, arts and humanities disciplines, where textual content is the focus of study as well as the mode of representation of learning, to other areas of the curriculum and into the STEM arena. The video essay demands a level of visual media literacy which, it can be reasonably argued, most students possess from their everyday curational practices and can thus be claimed as a meaning-making currency in contemporary culture, perhaps at odds with, or at least requiring more strategic alignment with, the more 'logocentric' modes of assessment favoured by the academy. So dominant is the written mode that the ever-increasing expansion of more creative and visual assessment design continues to be 'reined in' by validation panels requiring metrics of equivalence to written word ranges:

Composing a video essay for assessment purposes is not a soft option, especially in a pedagogic context that is obsessed with data, metrics and measurable learning outcomes that testify to a student's mastery of disciplinary knowledge, skills and capabilities. The point is that writing with sound and vision is still an exercise in writing, which is why we in the academy need to expand our conception of writing.

(D'Cruz, 2021, p 63)

The video essay is not distinctly an online learning modality, but the use of YouTube to upload video not only for assessment and peer review but also for a potentially open audience makes it a form of assessment design that has obvious benefits in the virtual context. But it also offers a bridging format, as the work is 'still' an essay, as opposed to a more radical departure from the dominant practice. The use of video and words together, edited and motivated for multiple contexts does, however, provide a reflexive decon-struction that speaks to constructivist principles, drawing on auto and digital ethnographies and assessment for learning towards a realisation of praxis, argue Fowler and Redmond, who offer the video essay as a counter-hegemonic assessment design:

For a radical pedagogy, the only way to see what's outside the box is to demateri-alise its structures and forces and to simultaneously reimagine the very way that learning takes place.

(2021, p 7)

Summary

This chapter has explored:

- the affordances of online assessment with regard to the enduring Vygotskian principles for constructive alignment and constructivist feedback loops;

- more complex territory raising critical questions about data, learning analytics and ed-tech proctoring;

- the discursive intersection of standards and performance in the broader sense.

Useful texts

Carless, D (2020) From Teacher Transmission of Information to Student Feedback Literacy: Activating the Learner Role in Feedback Processes. *Active Learning in Higher Education*. [online] Available at: https://doi.org/10.1177/1469787420945845 (accessed 2 June 2021).

Important reference point for online assessment from a prominent figure in assessment research.

Curtis, A (2021) Can't Get You Out of My Head. [online] Available at: www.bbc.co.uk/iplayer/episodes/p093wp6h/cant-get-you-out-of-my-head (accessed 2 June 2021).

This documentary is thought-provoking and raises important questions about tech-nology, ideas, the inner mind and civic structures that are pertinent for higher education and how it assesses itself and its students and how students assess its functions in the digital media ecosystem.

Journal of Media Practice and Education, 22:1 Special Issue: The Audio-visual Essay as Creative Practice in Teaching and Research: Theories, Methods, Case Studies. [online] Available at: www.tandfonline.com/toc/rjmp20/current (accessed 2 June 2021).

A series of articles and linked media from the case study in the chapter.

Surrey Assessment and Learning Lab: *Feedback Opportunities in Online Learning.* [online] Available at: www.surrey.ac.uk/sites/default/files/2020-05/feedback-covid_46121451%20%289%29.pdf (accessed 2 June 2021).

Info-graphic to help connect online feedback modes to purpose, with a range of links.

*Educational environments should be spaces that facilitate
engaged, critical and empowered thinking and action that
aim to address societal issues.*

(Gabriel, 2019, p 1460)

*You're an intelligent AF [Artificial Friend]. Maybe you
can see things the rest of us can't. Maybe you're right
to be hopeful, Maybe you're right.*

(Ishiguro, 2021, p 108)

To what extent can online learning environments, the social practices that take place in them and the socio-material dynamics in play in and around them redistribute power for equality, diversity and inclusion, and how does online make a difference to these things, specifically?

It is useful to return to questions asked in my previous work (Potter and McDougall, 2016).

>> What happens to people doing education in a (digital) third space?

>> How do engagements in the (digital) third space influence practices back in the second space?

… but then to rephrase for this book.

Critical questions for practice

>> How can what happens to people doing education in the online (third) space more equal, diverse and inclusive than it was in the second, and what makes it so?

>> Can the different relations and dynamics at work in online teaching compared to physical campus presence be an opportunity for you to make these spaces differently and better?

> » Can online education promote social justice without directly challenging inequalities, without *'Teaching to Transgress'* (hooks, 1994)?
>
> » Does this work demand learning contexts that deconstruct power dynamics and oppression in education as its own object. In other words, is there now an element of the study of education in itself within all disciplines – a meta, reflexive deconstruction of the conditions of possibility for the subject?

3D pedagogy

The principles of '3D pedagogy' – diversity, democracy, decolonialisation (Gabriel, 2020) – offer a conceptual framing for an assessment of how online learning in higher education relates to feminism, critical race theory, social class, post-colonial, intersectional approaches and post-humanism and how these perspectives, political objectives and international contexts can 'decentre' the social practices of higher education, potentially.

Critical question for practice

> » When, and how, does online learning in higher education enable critical pedagogy?

Gabriel's necessary challenge is to see intersectional marginalisation as a first principle. As Whiteness and maleness continue to trade with rich capital dividends, learning and teaching in online spaces can only be *more* inclusive for social justice if it starts out from a deconstruction of these *'interlocking systems of privilege and oppression'* (Douglas, 2017, p 50). Kwhali describes the lived experience of the 'accidental academic' without the means to trade Whiteness:

I will never entirely reconcile the personal and political meaning of my race, class and gender within a higher education setting constructed around the epistemology of whiteness, maleness and class divisions ... None of the institutions at which I have worked has attempted to understand how racial aloneness is experienced or how the knowledge that arises from my gender and race co-exists alongside the need to satisfy the white criteria of meaning.

(Kwhali, 2017, pp 5–21)

As the broader and applied imperatives of Black Lives Matter and 'Why is My Curriculum White?' have cast a critical lens, we see through it that the habitus clash described above by Kwhali, for whom it's not just about being in a White space, but also about learning White knowledge, the combination of ontology and epistemology.

At the heart of the contemporary crisis (a reasonable term to describe the situation) in UK universities over so-called 'cancel culture' and new debates over free speech is an epistemological disruption. While Baggini, in a recent attempt to provide a global account of philosophy, but starting out from the West, observes:

At a societal level – if not the individual level – there are always some justifications for beliefs which carry more weight than others; reasons why some things are accepted as true and others rejected as false. Every culture has an implicit, folk epistemology – a theory of knowledge – just as almost every philosophy has an explicit one and these formal and informal epistemologies are connected.

(Baggini, 2018, p 26)

Kehinde Andrews (2017) argues that the reproduction of Enlightenment philosophy across the curriculum as neutral and universal *in itself* produces racism:

We should have long ago put to bed the myth that there is any history of Britain that does not include the stories of the darker peoples from the colonies. Truly decolonising the curriculum would entail deconstructing the Eurocentric basis for our study of history. Tinkering at the edges will not solve this crisis of knowledge.

Critical theory has long argued over notions of 'the different' (Lyotard, 1994) where micropolitical idioms in language games are respected for ethics of difference, at the risk of relativism which can arguably be seen to be played out in our 'post-truth' environment in the twenty-first century. But Andrews' intervention is concerned with the daily lived experience of how universities impose formal epistemologies. The project of decolonising knowledge in online spaces is about 'epistemological ecumenicalism' (Onwuegbuzie, 2002), whereby situated, indigenous theory-building from the Global South informs Western epistemologies, constructed through partnership as social, convivial and plural, as opposed to colonial and hierarchical (Nyamnjoh, 2017).

Critical question for practice

» How can we use the affordances of online learning for the principles of 3D pedagogy – diversity, democracy, decolonialisation – while safeguarding against appropriating this way of working in online spaces as a reductive 'approach'?

Returning to Deborah Gabriel's work, at the core of her *Transforming the Ivory Tower* project is the capacity to act – *'how to transform the spaces we work in and how to transform ourselves'* (Gabriel, 2020, p 2). As universities responded, within months, to both the pandemic and the murder of George Floyd, we could reasonably expect her *3D pedagogy* objectives (decolonising, democratising and diversifying the curriculum) to move inward from the margins, given the opportunity presented to re-design learning and teaching and deconstruct the conditions of possibility for knowledge and curriculum, with students as partners, the same students who were galvanised by Black Lives Matter for the most part.

However, this is dangerous thinking, even an appropriation, in its 'fast track', solutionist way of thinking about a sustained, situated response to epistemological racism (see Tuhiwai-Smith, 2012), claiming a space for agency within the structure as a 'quick fix'. Instead, the dialogic pedagogy that embeds 3D as a collective mindset requires long-term community building:

Equity requires recognition of the social, cultural, political, and economic benefits that White privilege has brought people racialised as White for centuries, through systemic racism. Equity necessitates that positive actions are taken to redress the racial advantage of whiteness before equality can be achieved. Racial equality cannot be achieved without racial equity.

(Gabriel, 2020, p 167)

Allies for social justice recognize the interconnectedness of oppressive structures and work in partnership with marginalized persons toward building social justice coalitions. They aspire to move beyond individual acts and direct attention to oppressive processes and systems. Their pursuit is not merely to help oppressed persons but to create a socially just world.

(Patton and Bondi, 2015, p 490)

Gabriel's colleagues in the Black British Academics network write about the methods required for such spaces to be productive for levelling work, collectivism, protest and action. These are participatory, reflexive and non-hierarchical. These ways of being together in and against the academy – *'learning to work through the pain we feel'* – are about taking approaches to transformational social justice pedagogy into actions that instil social justice in every conversation about learning in universities, for all of us who benefit materially from interlocking power structures to shift from reflective to *reflexive*, from pedagogic practice to *praxis*, to dismantle the normative criteria we use in the curriculum, rather than just critique them but carry on regardless.

Critical questions for practice

» How do online learning dynamics conceptualised typically as spaces at least provide an opportunity for a praxis of redress?

» How do the pedagogic principles at work in these online spaces put into play a dismantling of epistemological power?

The attainment gap (of almost 25 per cent) between White and Black and Minority Ethnic (BAME) undergraduates achieving a first-class degree or higher second, as required for progression to postgraduate study, inevitably leads to a lack of diverse visibility in academic work and this is combined with both financial impediments to access at all levels and the well-rehearsed hegemonic school curriculum that 'keeps another gate'. In this 360 arena of inequality, online learning cannot be a panacea, and in addition to the inconvenient (but obvious) truth that digital inequalities replicate all the others, there are risks of more or less conscious assumptions about students of colour being somehow more comfortable online as though the internet is a neutral 'safe space' for 'non-traditional entrants' to the academy:

Women, ethnic minorities, younger people, and those with fewer socio-economic resources historically have less access to formal social capital. It is mostly their lack of this formal social capital, rather than their lack of skills, interests or economic resources, that drives inequalities in digital civic engagement.

(Helsper, 2021, p 113)

Using Sen's capability approach (2008) to evaluate online learning for social justice, we can understand this in terms of the degree of success in developing human capability from resources to functioning to access to learning, to explore this new combination of practices within '*a mesh of interconnections*' (Livingstone and Sefton-Green, 2016, p 61). Capability, in Sen's terms, emphasises human diversity, the significance of choice-making and the possibilities of flourishing, and *can* provide a conduit for social praxis and the *potential* to give voice and address marginality. Tait (2013) linked open learning to social justice through Sen's framework in an attempt to better define how social justice is understood in relation to development in a social and political context. Tait's analysis confirmed that universities at the time with significant intentions to use open e-learning for development were primarily focussed on social justice through access and flexibility:

These affordances above all deliver flexibility regarding time and place that permits study alongside work and family; includes people in geographies that would otherwise be excluded; supports the inclusion of women where independent movement to study on a campus is restricted, and of the house bound, the disabled, and the imprisoned for whom study on the campus is not possible; it can permit study by individuals otherwise excluded by cost where distance and e-learning has been able to lower cost as against other educational systems; and through scale can provide opportunities for far more people than would otherwise be possible.

(Tait, 2013, p 5)

In going forward from this situation to positioning the capability framework as a lens through which to view online learning's social justice intentionalities in higher education, Tait moves us towards a place where we can see things as a whole, access and then participate, and with the capability to activate change.

Example 4.1

Kaleidoscope network

The Kent Law School's *Decolonising the Curriculum* project (University of Kent, 2020) is not specific to online activity but makes rich use of Soundcloud for an audio campus walk which is clearly transferable as an activity for students. The kaleidoscope network principles are stated as follows: check our White (and other) privileges, actively listen (don't speak yet!), actively learn (read and reflect), reflect more (sit with, and breathe through, discomfort) and time to act (anti-racist solidarity work). The online materials provided by the network can easily be used with students on any programme at any level as a set of protocols for working together on a module's activities and towards learning outcomes while, at the moment, decolonising the curriculum 'from within'. This might, and that can only be tentatively stated in a book by a White, male author, support the movement from good intentions to restorative practice:

It does not matter that the 'intentions' of individual educators were noble. Forget about intentions. What any institution or its agents, 'intend' for you is secondary ... The point of this language of 'intention' and 'personal responsibility' is broad exoneration. Mistakes were made. Bodies were broken. People were enslaved. We meant well. We tried our best. 'Good intention' is a hall pass through history, a sleeping pill that ensures the Dream.

(Coates, 2015, p 33)

Critical issues

'Culture wars'?

During the production of this book, the UK Government announced plans to appoint a 'Free Speech Tsar' for universities. A disclaimer, then, that the implementation of this agenda and the lived experience of it in the sector was 'to be confirmed' at the time of writing. This came after a protracted tussle over several years over the increasing use of trigger warnings in unit guides, the concept of 'safe space' and the contested policy of no-platforming by student unions at UK universities. Following the 'no platforming' at the University of Cambridge of Linda Bellos and the English department's trigger warnings at the same institution, the ethical and political fault-lines between respect for students' (and academics') trans identities and the concerns articulated by 'trans-exclusionary' radical feminists took centre stage in an argument over no-platforming which was later extended to the removal of statues and the renaming of buildings associated with Britain's colonial and slave trade history. The term 'woke', initially a positive marker for an awakening to a commitment to social justice and openness to reparation for historical wrongs, became equivalent to the discursive framing of attempts to deal with marginalising language as 'political correctness' and was extended to a moral panic over 'cancel culture'. All of this speaks to a broader, long-standing argument over the role of the university in free speech and the discussion of sensitive issues. One person's 'cancel culture' is another's 'flagging up' of sensitive issues ahead of events (this is how students' union representatives see the policy of trigger warnings, for example) and one person's cautionary, pragmatic 'self-censorship' – an act of risk aversion rather than acceptance of erosion of free speech, perhaps – is another's removal of the *critical* questions this series foregrounds. The UK Government legislation is designed to give rights to legal action for the 'no-platformed' and to link funding and Office for Students regulation to a set of conditions for free speech in universities, with a direct remit for students' unions to comply.

Critical question for practice

» Where is the evidence of online learning in higher education enabling an open, honest 'brave space' to challenge Enlightenment epistemology?

The field of media and digital literacy research has reached a maturation stage where the community is able to focus more on the intersectional, lived experiences of digital practices than neutral measures of skills or competencies, the shift from thinking about literacy as static to literacies as dynamic. Part of this trajectory has located digital literacies within a broader understanding of capability – civic, educational, professional, the uses of literacy, the social practices of being literate, in context. Helsper (2021) advocates for a meso-level approach to digital agencies to understand stratification of capability as 'socio-digital':

Socio-digital inequalities should be defined as inequalities in the achievement of positive outcomes and the avoidance of negative outcomes of ICT use in digital societies. Socio-digital inequalities are systematic differences between individuals from different backgrounds in the opportunities and abilities to translate digital engagement into benefits and avoid the harm that might result from engagement with ICTs. To understand the barriers and enablers to overcoming socio-digital inequalities requires taking a compound approach that includes access, skills, attitudes and different ways of engaging with ICTs. This approach must be relative, understanding how the economic, social and cultural environments in which a person spends time shape their perceptions of how important digital engagement is.

(Helsper, 2021, p 44)

There is no suggestion here that anything about digital practices by themselves bring social justice or decolonisation into play, that should be obvious. Rather, the practices might be enabled or enhanced by the digital, as McLean shows in her account of using immersive media to build decolonial moments – operative terms being *use* and *build*, or '*using troublesome tools for constructive ends*' (2021, p 14). Sharing her practice in a Digital Humanities context of working with students in immersive media contexts to decentre Global North epistemologies, McLean is very careful to guard against modes of practice which ignore the troublesome nature of platform colonialism in the form of Google Classroom, for example. As Andrews (2021, p 164) puts it, we must be awake to the fact that '*a cottage industry has developed around imagining salvation in the form of western techno-logical development*', so it would be an extraordinary act of 'strategic ignorance' (McGoey, 2019) to think that using such technologies for the pursuit of redistri-bution will not be fraught with tensions. The work to be done, instead, is to work with the tools in a critical, decolonial framing, using Fanon's (1963) strategy for disorder:

The embodied experiences afforded by digital technologies play a role in the efficacy of immersive media in terms of helping students develop deeper insights about indigenous ontologies and epistemologies .... By offering learning and teaching opportunities that focus on indigenous knowledges and explicitly critique colonial histories and presences with immersive media experiences, decolonial learning moments were experienced that may contribute to broader programs of unsettling colonial power.

(McLean, 2021, p 15)

Example 4.2

Every Learner Everywhere

Every Learner Everywhere (ELE, see www.everylearnereverywhere.org/equity/) is an organisation with the stated mission to '*help universities use new technology to innovate teaching and learning, with the ultimate goal of improving student outcomes for Black, Latinx, and Indigenous students, poverty-affected students, and first-generation students*'. The project sets out to bust a number of myths and provide resources for thinking differently, including the assumption that '*digital learning is the solution for inequity in digital learning*'; that 'evidence-based' teaching practices are always equitable; that in digital learning environments there is no way for students to be judged on their race or gender. Moving from dismantling these myths to resources for action, higher education practitioners can apply the resources to address disparities, mitigate the negative effects of implicit bias awareness and understand, in order to change, *'the key things that universities get wrong when it comes to using technology equitably'*. ELE's *AntiRacist Practices for Digital and Online Learning* materials could offer a critical thinking 'safe space' for everyone involved in a unit or module before agreeing to embed the Kent network principles in ways of working together.

Critical question for practice

» How can our work in online higher education be informed by a meso-level understanding of digital inequalities?

Community-building: the 'Brave Space'

OneHE's Equity Unbound resources offer pedagogic strategies for community building to reduce the risks of marginalisation in everyday learning and teaching practices. For example, 'Thick Greetings' sets out to provide a 'slower, thicker and more deliberate opportunity' for class interactions, similar to the 'complex personhood mapping' described previously in the Contemporary Perspectives case study. A social justice self-assessment tool invites educational practitioners to *'Gauge your level of competence and comfort in the themes of gender-consciousness, interculturalism, and community, both in their individual pedagogical practices and wider academic engagements'* (Bali, 2021).

Continuing to add these examples as building blocks, the critical issue here is that the transfer of intentions into online praxis requires community building and sub-community interactions in digital spaces, or a community of communities, so the recommendation is about adding the Equity Unbound online activities to the Every Learner Everywhere 'mindset space' and the Kent network principles.

For lecturers, the University of Wisconsin's resources for anti-racist and inclusive teaching in online contexts go further to directly address the intersectional impacts of Covid as family income reductions are disproportionate to already disadvantaged groups and LGBTQ students reported additional problems in lockdowns, and to bear witness to the university's cohort being, in many cases, directly involved in protests:

As instructors, we can be pro-active and make our make our classrooms more anti-racist, more inviting to our students whose communities have been under attack, and more responsive to the call for racial justice.

(University of Wisconsin–Oshkosh, 2020)

The activities and approaches shared link three strands of pedagogic practice: designing learning and assessment that addresses these current issues; facilitating an inclusive and equitable 'brave space' for students; and moving forward more broadly as an anti-racist educator in online modes.

Critical question for practice

» How can we work with 'troublesome tools' for social justice objectives?

Example 4.3

Decolonising online development studies

While several of the examples in this chapter, and indeed throughout the book, are about how online dynamics offer new and different opportunities for ways of working with students and between academics that could and do also happen in face to face interactions, Spiegel et al's (2017) contribution speaks to the example of online development studies programmes led by Western universities with students in low-income countries to ask '*Can e-learning creatively work towards a decolonising agenda that meaningfully confronts Western institutional hegemonies and power imbalances in development studies?*' The research found that the access provided by online learning was only partially followed through to critical pedagogy and only partially successful in addressing Global South discourse imposition with regard to international development, so an example that might appear to 'lend itself' more readily to the connection of online learning to social justice community knowledge generation is just as fraught with tensions and risk:

Students were invited to reflect on various kinds of academic expertise when challenging notions of 'expertise' in prescriptive development policy analysis – to challenge both the framing of 'problems' and the framing of 'solutions' as well as the wider linear logics – by, for example, drawing mind-maps with multiple webs of social relation and chains of causality and posting them online, to challenge entrenched 'expert' narratives on environmental, health and economic issues. The teaching dilemmas encountered here also tapped into a much wider debate about whether a decolonising lens works at all in the context of student-practitioners who saw their task of learning as instrumental (for set institutional purposes) rather than as explicitly counter-hegemonic and anti-colonial.

(Spiegel et al, 2017, p 282)

Summary

This chapter has worked through:

- the potential for online learning to disrupt pedagogic and epistemological ways of being in higher education for reasons of social justice and equity;

- where the online domain can unsettle things for these important reasons, and how we can embrace this – as we must.

Useful texts

Gabriel, D with McDougall, J (2020) Can We Talk? A White, Middle Class Male's Perspective on *Transforming the Ivory Tower: Models for Gender Equality & Social Justice*, through the Black Feminist Approach of Participatory Witnessing. *Media Practice and Education*, 21(3).

A critical conversation between the author of this book and Deborah Gabriel, on the themes of this chapter, necessarily unsettling for the former.

University of Kent (2020) *Kaleidoscope Network – Decolonising the University.* [online] Available at: https://research.kent.ac.uk/sergj/kaleidoscope-network-decolonising-the-university/ (accessed 2 June 2021).

As suggested in the chapter, using the network principles here, informed by the full set of materials, in connection with other online resources and pedagogic strategies can offer a useful set of 'building blocks'.

Equity Unbound – *Social Justice Self-Assessment Tool*. [online] Available at: https://onehe.org/eu-activity/self-assessment-tool-of-social-justice-in-your-teaching-from-discs-disciplines-inquiring-into-societal-challenges/ (accessed 2 June 2021).

A starting point for 'safe space' reflection on our own practices and consciousness with regard to the texts we select, the diversity of our students and our awareness of the colonial roots of our work.

Spiegel, S, Gray, H, Bompani, B, Bardosh, K and Smith, J (2017) Decolonising Online Development Studies? Emancipatory Aspirations and Critical Reflections – A Case Study. *Third World Quarterly*, 38(2): 270–90.

A very useful case study on the complexity of medium and message, perhaps asking more questions than providing answers, but with those questions being importantly critical.

Williams, J (2020) *Anti-Racist Practices for Digital and Online Learning*. [online] Available at: www.youtube.com/watch?v=zkOT1l3uGzQ (accessed 21 September 2020).

Self-explanatory, it can be assumed at this point.

Chapter 5 | Newman now: the desituated soul

In this chapter, John Henry Newman's formative work *The Idea of a University* (1899) is reimagined. The approach taken in keeping with the previous reappraisals from the 'line of sight' of Roland Barthes, Charles Dickens, Raymond Williams and Richard Hoggart (see Bennett and McDougall, 2013, 2016a, 2016b and Bennett et al, 2020) is to think not *'in character as "Newman today" but within Newman's conceptual framework'*.

Newman's text has often cited a foundation for the kind of personalised, student-centred, *comprehensive* experience the UK university struggles to provide in a now fully marketised sector:

Hence it is that education is called 'Liberal.' A habit of mind is formed which lasts through life, of which the attributes are, freedom, equitableness, calmness, moderation, and wisdom; or what in a former Discourse I have ventured to call a philosophical habit. This then I would assign as the special fruit of the education furnished at a University, as contrasted with other places of teaching or modes of teaching. This is the main purpose of a University in its treatment of its students.

(Newman, 1996, p 77)

Much of this, and everything that has been covered up to now in this book, hinges on what we think about when we think about a university and what happens when it is online, and whether higher education is a set of social practices within a university, on campus or virtual, or whether it is something else. The 'in-between' question is posted by Dave White at the University of the Arts, London (UAL) – asking *'how we might reimagine, rather than replicate, our institutions online'*. For White, we need to be thinking about the desituated ontology of, in his frame of reference, the art school, but more broadly, the university:

The physical building, and the teaching modes associated with it, are still what defines 'teaching' even when we are fully online. Online is not yet conceptualised as a teaching location in its own right when students are taking part in what is considered to be a face-to-face course, even when the design of the course involves a significant amount of online activity.

(White, 2020)

This is not the first recontextualising of Newman's idea for the digital age. Landow (1996) discussed the implications of hypertext for relational thinking and 'virtual presence' within campus practices and rightly took issue with Newman's disparaging remarks about mass literacy. In his analysis, however, he moves on to argue that Newman would have come to see aspects of the digital democratisation of knowledge as useful contributions to students' investment in learning and the interdisciplinary thinking he advocated for, as will be covered in this chapter. With regard to the idea of the virtual university *itself*, Landow's critical questions are similar to our concerns a quarter of a century on:

Newman thought that the university would nurture virtues by means of a kind of ethos. Will that sense of the university as a place of values survive a university that is not in a single place? Furthermore, the sense of a university as a place has often nurtured students' personal development. Will the digital university destroy that nurturing?

(Landow, 1996, pp 358–9)

The discourse precepts for higher education in 2021 have delimited the sayable to situate universities as being businesses in a market, competing for students as customers; variably worthy of investment funds for research and obliged to pursue the development of their outputs for societal impact and commercial exploitation. The proliferation of data and metrics for performance management span the value for money of teaching as well as research, with the student as a consumer and their graduate employment a commodity with exchange value.

Recently, analyses of 'neoliberal' discourse in the era of polarisation and populism observe that the 'liberal' solution, Newman's legacy, to inequality and poverty *wrongly* positions education as the antidote when its function has always been to perpetuate it (see also Peim, 2016), but in a constant state of pathological denial:

Ultimately, by producing and maintaining the failed meritocracy, neoliberal liberals end up supporting inequality and poverty, but they cannot recognize this connection because they are so invested in seeing themselves as doing good, and they reject any criticism that would shatter their idealized self-image. Fundamentally, meritocratic narcissism is based on the desire to engage in competitive capitalism without having to feel any guilt for the losers of the system.

(Samuels, 2016, p 32)

Those in the academy who wish to cling to some of Newman's ideals in the neoliberal environment are deluded, for Samuels and Peim, complicit in replacing overtly political activism with an *illusion* of educational meritocracy. This is manifested most frequently in discursive framings such as 'new pedagogies', 'co-creation', 'students as partners', 'fair access', 'widening participation', 'student voice', 'global engagement', 'employability' and 'graduate attributes', all of which serve to perpetuate the empty signifier of the 'student experience'.

If so, then any concluding hypothesis for the 'university of the future' as a blended, at least partly, virtual *experience* of higher education, if not a place or a space, as such, where it takes place, cannot evade such critical questions. A return to Newman calls.

In 1852, Newman wrote that the function of a university was to teach universal knowledge, and that knowledge is valuable and important for its own sake and not just for its perceived value to society.

In 2021, *Times Higher Education* convened a webinar panel on 'Creating the universities of the future today' an academia–industry partnership with Desire 2 Learn (D2L), a global software company that provides a virtual learning environment procured by the UK universities. Something of a 'grand narrative' was emerging at the time of this panel, regarding the consensus that we were never going back, or as the Open University's John Domingue put it '*the online genie was out of the bottle, forever*' (in Doughty, 2021).

Futuring #1

The *THE* panel discussion, between Tim McIntyre-Bhatty (Bournemouth University), Jason Last (University College, Dublin), Stewart Watts (D2L) and Jonathan Eaton (Teesside University), covered the need for a blended future, as universities 'keep pace with the digital revolution' while maintaining the essential attributes of the campus premium, articulated by the panellists in terms of people, place and identity. McIntyre-Bhatty called for universities to distinguish between what we can do and what we should do, with echoes of the science fiction trope running through *Frankenstein* to *Blade Runner*, *Jurassic Park*, *Zed* (and the thematically linked BBC series *Devs*) and right up to *Klara and the Sun* (these intertextual references are my interpretation) and reminded the audience about 'the sticky campus'. Last and Watts addressed fitness for purpose and the required 'upskilling' of academics, the D2L perspective being:

I think everybody has realised that good online learning looks very, very different to good face-to-face learning. It requires different types of content to drive engagement. The design of the course structure is completely different ... it's a whole new pedagogy that has had to be learned.

At the furthest departure from Newman's line of sight, the panel discussed data analytics and the need for a two-way street, with institutions using data to capture signs for disengagement retention risks and design pedagogies around 'personalisation analytics' but also agreeing that students need to be stakeholders in a 'radical transparency' of data visibility – asking another key critical question about data surveillance – 'what's in it for students?' What Newman would make of the idea that a university's 'operating methodology' should be student-driven so that they can optimise performance for outcomes from their degree is definitely a known unknown, but for our purposes here, there is perhaps an interesting complexity around the intentionality for the architecture of datafied blended learning in higher education to provide manifestations of constructivist learning theories. The example that follows takes a deeper dive into this issue with one of the *THE* panellists.

Example 5.1

Fusion

Following up with Tim McIntyre-Bhatty is useful, as his 'Fusion' model can be reasonably seen to exemplify radical transparency in the strategic intersecting of education, research and professional practice across all aspects of university activity, every course, every student's experience and every academic's work planning and development. Thinking directly now about Newman's 'idea', whereas the *THE* panel dialogue had resonated with some of the philosophical underpinnings, he reflects on a decade of investment, across all sectors of education, in devices and connectivity that enable data and information to be accessed at 'next to zero cost' in terms of both time and money. But he is also open about the slow development by universities, pedagogically, in the data information–knowledge equation and sees the online pivot necessitated by Covid as pressing that issue. The challenge, for the pursuit of truth, in Newman's terms, is the pedagogies needed to convert information into knowledge and to work with the balance of intended benefits and unintended risks from doing so. How universities enable learning within that fine balance to be deserving of public trust in using digital in new ways is a question of values, he says. This is profoundly educator-led, partly a matter of 'team by team' discipline negotiation but also partly a matter of market segmentation and differentiation. The product universities offer is experiential and cannot be universal, even if the place of learning is virtual, or at least blended.

Newman's Enlightenment view of darkness and light, ignorance and truth is, of course, deeply problematic to set up a foundational text straight after consideration of decolonising and anti-racist work in online spaces. His *ex umbris et imaginibus in vertitatem!* (from shadows and symbols into truth) cannot be conveniently deployed at the service of attacking neoliberal higher education while side-stepping the legacy of Eurocentric erasure of 'other' truths.

Brookfield (2005) provided a compelling set of strategies for a critical theory-informed pedagogy, characterised by an interplay of reproduction and opposition – echoing the work of Paul Willis in the past and McIntyre-Bhatty in the future-facing present – at the heart of the pedagogic challenge:

Critical theory is normatively grounded in a vision of a society in which people live collectively in ways that encourage the free exercise of their creativity without foreclosing that of others. In such a society people see their individual well-being as integrally bound up with that of the collective. They act toward each other with generosity and compassion and are ever alert to the presence of injustice, inequity and oppression. Creating such a society can be understood as entailing a series of learning tasks: learning to recognise and challenge ideology that attempts to portray the exploitation of the many by the few as a natural state of affairs, learning to overcome alienation and thereby accept freedom, learning to pursue liberation, learning to reclaim reason and learning to practice democracy.

(Brookfield, 2005, p 39)

Futuring #2 (Newman)

Back to 'Newman Now', in March 2021, I discussed these ideas with a group of academics (see Figure 5.1), whose contributions on critical approaches to online learning have been discussed already for this project: John Potter from UCL, Debbie Holley from Bournemouth University, Sarah Jones from De Montfort University, Leicester, and Dave White from UAL whose thinking kick-started this chapter and provided its title. We considered Newman's writing about higher education being primarily a matter of cultivating, or even 'perfecting', the intellect and this endeavour being fundamental to the soul of a university. With some echoes of postmodern/posthuman questions about the possibility of thought without a body, I asked the panellists if Newman's 'soul of the university' can live on without a campus.

Sarah: *My 'heart' belongs to my first university, where I did my undergraduate degree. And that's because of the transformative experiences, living away from home, the ideas that were formed but also growing and developing, networking and the huge array of opportunities that a university gives. When I think about that now, even in an online environment, there is still a soul, still that idea of what a university is, it's still that holistic approach, still that pivotal moment for a student, that's what you relate to later on in reflection, that transformation, but it can exist online or offline.*

John: *I think the soul is located in the physical space. The actual place, the campus of Leeds University, for me, it felt like you were going somewhere with ideals, it did have an environment, it did have an atmosphere, it did have an identity. The space to develop in other ways, forming bands, going to gigs, it's all wrapped up in place. What's really interesting is the situation since March 2020, the impossibility of recreating that space online, it doesn't happen. The online experience is different but is not 'the place'.*

Dave: *I would argue that the concept of place has been interestingly complicated over the past 30 years. The university isn't a set of buildings, it's the work of the university, it's the way we engage the students, it's the research and the teaching. The place of the university still exists as a concept but it's less tied to the buildings now, everyone involved in the place making of the university now might not be located geographically at the university. The buildings are an extremely powerful embodiment of a set of ideas, sometimes too powerful. The interesting thing about Newman is that it's very progressive but also radically exclusive. I love buildings, but I think buildings are fundamentally exclusive, so I think we need to evolve the concept of the place of the university to include the desituated soul and we should be honest that the sector was already there pre-Covid and if you don't consider it along these lines then you risk this dangerous dislocation between what people consider to be the real university and then bits that are bolted onto it. Covid might well have broken that in a way that could be useful if we are prepared to think about the relationship between place and location differently. In terms of what universities want to be, de-situated is an aspiration, international students, partnerships, greater fluidity, not being tied to geography. What does it mean to be, not place agnostic, but location agnostic?*

Debbie: *The elitism of Newman's ideas jar with me. But also, the neoliberal agenda has dislocated the soul. The lived reality of the soul has been squeezed out with metrics, data, the regulatory environment and the lack of differentiation. The soul of a university should be much less elitist and much more embedded in local and civic society, in the way that Illich talked about those notions of community.*

The discussion here resonated with the critical questions about Enlightenment and decolonising our work above and in Chapter 4. What did the panellists think about the

Figure 5.1 Zoom panel.

possibility that the situatedness of higher education, in the metaphysics of presence on campus spaces, plays a role in the habitus anxiety experienced in the colonial framing of both knowledge and university space? Can online higher education move us away from the colonial trappings of Newman's idea?

Debbie: *I want to jump in and scream! It's not a neutral, value-free space; all of the societal inequalities still play out there, in the online space.*

John: *My first answer was a nostalgic looking back and many of us went to university on full grants, of course, so let's bring it up to date. The idea of a university has been colonised itself by market forces and neoliberalism so we are engaged in a struggle here. We have to think about how the essence of what our university represented can be communicated on pedagogy and through the materials we use to decolonise the curriculum but it won't happen without effort and struggle and online environments have doors and windows too, passwords, access to resources, access to hardware to access the resources. The re-advantaging of learners that you can get online, the microteaching and workshop stuff, not content delivery. The desituated soul work is really important but it doesn't happen 'because online'.*

Dave: *There's a utopian thread to this idea that moving online is somehow liberating. And I agree that these spaces aren't neutral. Who owns the space? There is all kinds of new colonisation going on which is, again, not geographically demarcated. When we consider physical space, people are very precise about who owns it, who has control over it, the right to shape it, who has access to it, what are the modes of engagement? Higher education has been very successfully colonised now by technology, in spaces we don't own but we just use. So we need to re-appropriate these spaces. And technology has outstripped us in terms of what its allows us to do and reflects back our own habits of replicating culture in particular ways. This technology allows us to talk to the whole world at once in theory but there is still very little fully open practice going on, which would more fully replicate our values and rhetoric, but what we are struggling with now is this massive potential flexibility that the technology gives us but also this desire to hang on to the structures of the university as we know them now. So, how do we reimagine the institution online rather than replicate it, and how do we that in ways that decolonise rather than mirror or create new forms of colonisation?*

Debbie: *Ideas like Education 4.0 are out there, but we still haven't got open credits, a student can't take a class from somewhere else online next semester, we can't harness free-flowing structures as we're still independent money-making units, the market-place narration. Open Education Resources, distributed by Creative Commons, create institutional tensions when they are treated as commodified owned content.*

Sarah: *We are caught between tensions all the time, always between different things, and the shift to online really added to that. We have a virtual studio where students are making on Instagram and sharing with clients in digital spaces, but also we have those that are trying to deliver online how they always have, and the same question is there with decolonisation, it's about whether you can think about a university another way.*

Newman, perhaps more by implication, favoured an interdisciplinary approach to epistemological enquiry in what he described as 'knowledge in relation to learning':

Possessed of this real illumination, the mind never views any part of the extended subject-matter of Knowledge without recollecting that it is but a part, or without the associations which spring from this recollection. It makes every thing in some sort lead to every thing else; it would communicate the image of the whole to every separate portion; till that whole becomes in imagination like a spirit, every where pervading and penetrating its component parts, and giving them one definite meaning.

(Newman, 1996, p 100)

Is there evidence already or opportunities in the future for online learning in higher education to do this work?

Dave: *Again, this is where the technology allows us to do more than we are structurally capable of doing. There is a generation of students who understand that to have a meaningful impact on the world, it's going to have to be inter- or multi-disciplinary. They are beyond modern, in that sense. But it comes down to the question of what we claim we are providing and often as universities what we are selling is identity. Incoming students want to know who they are going to become and that's fair enough, but it will be expressed as a reflection of subject or discipline. As those students progress they come to an understanding that they want to make more fluid connections and become frustrated by the siloed nature of our courses. So yes, the digital environment liberates us from buildings and rooms because you just give someone a link and they can turn up but it's always in the context of the university as a site of becoming.*

Sarah: *I think there is that huge opportunity with online learning, the open lecture, group work and flexibility, but we are not there, we're still in that mindset, still reacting. We haven't had that moment to sit and reflect on this opportunity to transform learning, if we bring in emerging technology, augmented, immersive and simulated learning experiences. It's about capacity to innovate.*

Debbie: *We need to break free from the chains of the ILO (independent learning outcome). I would love to see us reconceptualising around societal wicked challenges. By all means come to us to be a graphic designer or a nurse or a geologist but we want you to be in a community of learners, in the Freirean sense, but reconceptualised for the twenty-first century.*

John: *We've also got to take a look at the structures inside universities, which replicate market forces outside, competing for students and resources, balancing the books and being good citizens in the neoliberal institution. So that we can create academic transfer across the silos, they are reinforced within universities, and the quality assurance side of things sometimes creates a structural inequality, an internal marketisation of academic life which means innovation suffers, retreating to what you know and keep your head down and deliver the content in the most efficient way. The really creative stuff has been done by people in small teams helping each other out in a kind of small village economy within the institution and then reaching out to the next village to say 'have you found this as well?' There's a job of work to be done, and a great willingness, but we do need to free ourselves from some shackles.*

This village metaphor seems to work on several levels. The collective nurturing to 'raise a child' is well known. But the village community is evoked in 'restorative practice' also, in ideas about building social capital through participatory learning and decision making, empathy and trust. There's also something in 'the village' that brings constructivist, collaborative knowledge generation to the fore, as default, as Morris testifies in an account of the pivot from 'chalkface' to screen: '*I make some teacher "noises" to ensure that the class is flowing, but almost everything I get students to do now involves them working together*' (Morris, 2021). Newman (1996) was thinking about individual students in 'the university' and we've moved here to a discussion about decolonised epistemic communities of collective practice in digital networks around and between desituated institutions, so at first glance, it might seem very different. On the other hand, he judges that a university is '*a place where inquiry is pushed forward, and discoveries verified and perfected, and rashness rendered innocuous, and error exposed, by the collision of mind with mind, and knowledge with knowledge*'? A version of that endures in what our panel are saying about the idea of a university without a campus and is there in the critical approaches we need to do online learning in higher education.

But the critical questions about the colonisation of higher education by 'ed-tech' present a much more direct challenge to Newman's 'idea'. Williamson and Hogan (2021, p 2) present compelling evidence of an acceleration and amplification of business logics pervading higher education, with 'pandemic privatisation' hiding in plain sight, as the pivot to online sidesteps academics' critical faculties in the pursuit of 'what works':

Framed as a form of 'emergency relief' during campus closures, education technologies were also presented as an opportunity for investment and profit-making, with the growing market of edtech framed as a catalytic enabler of long-term HE reconstruction and reform.

Futuring #3: the matrix reloaded?

The colonisation of higher education by digital platforms is small C as well as these Big C concerns. The small C creep is a symptom of a pragmatic need for the rapid 'what works' in a crisis overriding the critical mechanisms of people who are otherwise very exacting in their investment in how we do things, as Dave White discusses above. Or, as

Mark Carrigan expresses it, 'We Need to Talk about Zoom', because '*I worry that if we don't we will institutionalise Zoom, in other words establish ways of doing video conferencing, which will be hard to shift even if we all hate them*' (Carrigan, 2020).

Unpacking the interplay of small and big c/C tech-colonisation further, in media reporting by both the sector's trade journal, *Times Higher Education*, hosts of the first panel described in this chapter, and the apparently left-leaning *Guardian*, seemingly neutral descriptions of the challenges for universities in the digital space are recently abundant. O'Connor (2020) calls for universities to adopt user experience (UX) analytics, learning from the success of streaming services such as Netflix. While 'less ivory tower' is a democratising principle many will relish, there is no apparent concern for the colonisation of the university by platform capitalism in the argument for the sector to undertake a 'user experience overhaul'.

And here's John Naughton (2021) re-setting Newman's question:

What exactly are universities for in a digital age? And in particular what is the rationale for expensively gathering large numbers of young people in the same physical space to be taught using 800-year-old pedagogies when the pandemic has shown what the Open University demonstrated 50 years ago – that other ways of teaching and learning are possible?

Naughton infuriated the academic readers of his paper with this 'false binary', between either the oldest of old school lectures and the fully online OU model, but the more glaring issue was the lack of any discussion of the ramifications of '*bang! – suddenly everything is on Zoom*', given that the author is a well-published critic of Silicon Valley business models.

In the novel *Zed*, a dystopian 'Real Virtuality' is achieved by a predictive algorithm:

As the audience nodded along, like a cast of smiling puppets, Guy delivered his usual speech. He knew this speech very well, and its main tenet was that the future had once been a blank space, and people had once been able to understand it, and now it was no longer a blank space, because his lifechain could know it. The audience nodded and smiled, as the lifechain already knew they would.

(Kavenna, 2019, p 130)

Farnell (2021) locates online learning in HE as a site of conflict between academics' agile innovations with pleasant surprise at the affordances of virtual in the moment of crisis on the one hand and the 'digital dystopia' of '*abusive technologies that replace empowerment with enforcement*' on the other. One does not have to be a Luddite or left-leaning cynic to view the celebration of UX above or the rollout of exam proctoring with attendant surveillance with trepidation when we consider how the architects of digital content platforms tend to view human resources:

We must urgently re-capture academic technology and reject Big Edu-Tech systems. We must favour products that use standardised, Libre open-source software or, even better, software developed within our own institutions. Reinvesting in the ICT department is essential to bring technological innovation back to the universities where it started and where it belongs. Technology must shape teaching according to our highest moral values, not just efficiencies. We must show our students trust and we must respect their privacy, dignity and self-determination.

(Farnell, 2021)

Trust, again. This critical question is about more than political anxiety over private investments and returns in public institutions or Orwellian 'dystopia' over algorithms and UX, as it can be argued, of course, that the inflation of fees and the transition to higher education as a desituated consumer product represent the end-game for such debates. Rather, this concerns the importance of public trust in universities in the era of 'information disorder' (Wardle and Derakhshan, 2017) and the fragmentation of civic authority. This need for universities to be trusted emerged as an issue of consensus among the aforementioned *THE* panellists. If universities are late to the 'digital party' of UX and algorithms, as O'Connor observes, then one of our most important critical questions is whether it is the kind of party we want to attend:

The challenge is to create a more responsive version of the public sphere for the digital age, one which is not controlled by giant tech companies and which is genuinely participative. Like the climate, democracy is fast reaching a tipping point. If the opportunity for change is not seized, the worst aspects of the present malaise – disinformation, dark money and spiralling polarisation – could well push us beyond a point of no return.

(Geoghegan, 2020, p 306)

Working in from macro to micro and meso levels as this book has tried to, it is clear that there is no one 'online learning' now and no shared direction of travel for it in the future, but there can be more of a consensus around the sites of conflict now, soon and next. These are about the role of digital higher education in environmental sustainability (the pursuit of the 'ecoversity'); how we deal with the inevitable increase of datafication, personalised neurotech analytics, surveillance and the emergence of the 'smart campus'; the balance between the immersive affordances for learning from simulation experiences offered by artificial intelligence and the professional status of ourselves in that equation (see Bayne et al, 2020). One absolute truth here is that we will need to ask critical questions at every turn.

Regarding the ecoversity, following Geoghegan's alignment of the two crises, another false and complacent binary we are at risk of assuming is that between the harms of travel and presence and the 'greening' benefits of online. A study of the environmental impact of the UK lockdown on one university found that:

Online education holds potential to shift significant quantities of GHG (Green House Gas) emissions from the sector of higher education to households. In the case of this study this is evidenced by almost complete replacement of the carbon footprint of the University commute with the GHG emissions of at-home teaching/learning.

(Filimonau et al, 2020, p 9)

What game will the 'university of the future' bring to these sites of conflict? Can the workforce and its consumers bring about *'a reimagining that takes account not only of climate issues, but of social justice, radical pedagogy, cultural diversity and decolon-isation'* (Bayne et al, 2020, p 198)?

Example 5.2

Digital at the core

The 2030 'Digital Strategy Prioritisation Matrix' is a contribution to university leadership and the promotion of a 'transformational mindset' generated by Universities UK, Jisc, Emerge Education and Salesforce (an 'industry leader in technology and philanthropy'), within *Digital at the Core* (see Iosad, 2020). The matrix is configured with a Y-axis for financial imperatives (generating income and cutting costs) and an X-axis for moving from transactional to transformational activity, with the following combinations:

» *Generating income and transformational activity: Reaching new markets with mode-free (on-par online and physical delivery)*

» *Cutting costs and transformational activity: Replacing physical campus with digital*

» *Cutting costs and transactional: Workflow automation*

» *Generating income and transactional: Scaling up existing revenue streams (lift and shift)*

(Iosad, 2020, p 11)

While it would be unfair to suggest that *Digital at the Core* posits a technological salvationism, there is a pervading discourse of 'better use' of technology for digital 'delivery' and the enabling of a singular 'digital experience' that either imagines technology to be neutral or adopts what McGoey (2019) calls 'strategic ignorance' of this fundamental concern. This discourse can be read as part of an enduring narrative of scientific progress in Western ideology, the positive notion of 'Digital Transformations' *succeeding* in reducing inequalities in educational opportunities or *failing* to provide solutions to climate change, as we can see in the techno-fatalist environmental work of Elizabeth Kolbert (2021). Adopting another false binary between the use of technology for positive change versus its use for biased algorithms or another, between technology and 'Team Human' (Rushkoff, 2019) is hard to resist as a measure of how new tools can solve old problems of access and inequality if we use them right, but they are all problematic if articulated as 'the technology':

Scarcity is not the problem, inequality is, and if the new system is built by the same people who profit from the old, then it is lunacy to expect better technology to liberate the poor. It is particularly delusional to think that global inequality, or white supremacy in the flesh, could possibly be remedied by a reboot of Enlightenment narratives of progress.

(Andrews, 2021, p 179)

The scale and reach of digital inequalities are beyond a 'critical issue'. Institutional practices online and on campus are increasingly inextricable from socio-material threats to equality, diversity and inclusion, which are seemingly mundane but in lived experience must be addressed as a pre-requisite for decolonising curriculum work. For example, the 2021 Netflix film *Code Bias* explores how algorithmic bias in facial recognition breaches civil liberties and social justice. This is not a pedagogic issue, directly, except that the proliferation of AI adoption of this kind by universities would, if unchecked, skew access to our learning and teaching through the kinds of bias we could never accept from 'real' intelligence:

This isn't some troubling but abstract thought experiment. AI shapes our lives now. Coded Bias lists actual examples of algorithms already making decisions about your credit, your health, your housing, your college or job applications, even your access to possibility. The system holds in its hands your hope of a better life – and there's no appeal if the computer says no.

(Trenholm, 2021)

Projections such as *Digital at the Core* imagine the future in ways that are seemingly based on scientific rigour and trajectories from current trends and societal needs, but they are also performative. Just as Judith Butler has shown that gender exists only in its performance and is thus something we can 'trouble'; so, Oomen, Hoffman and Hajer argue that a dramaturgical analysis of 'futuring techniques' (such as those deployed in the 2030 framework) reveals the interplay of genre, narrative and staging in the *performance* of future, as *'the politics of the future revolve around who can make their imagined futures authoritative in the scenes and stages that matter'* (2021, p 15).

Summary

In this chapter we have considered the following critical ideas about higher education.

- When learning moves online, or is designed to be virtual or a blended fusion of digital and face to face, this is not a neutral space and the same degree of critical thinking needs to be in play as whenever students engage with learning practices on campuses.

- Perhaps more critical energy is needed, given the intensity of 'futuring' and the opportunities for market imperatives to challenge long-standing sector conventions, implications for working conditions and professional identities.

- Maybe 'the idea of the university' itself is at stake in the online environment.

This book has explored research and practice in online learning in higher education; how learning might be designed in online 'third spaces'; what we mean by virtual and what opportunities it brings for dynamic and relational digital practices; how assessment can be different with the affordances of networked media; what the online space might offer for the project of decolonising the curriculum; and what threats it poses if we take it as 'neutral'.

The questions asked within the 2030 *Digital Strategy Framework*, summarised above, are also critical, but they start out from a different place. The framework covers leadership, staff, business model and investment. Perhaps surprisingly, the questions posed in the framework that link most closely to the concerns of this book are in the business model section, since they focus the most on students and learning.

Here, to conclude this book and also to look ahead, they are the subject to critique of their premise, to ask a question of the question, via Newman's 'idea'.

Critical questions for practice

'Going forward'

2030 Framework question	The idea of a university	Critical question, now
» How will your students' needs and expectations change over the next decade and how can you provide a digital experience that will meet or exceed them?	» Should the 'digital experience' (re)enable the generation of knowledge as an end in itself? And if so, how?	» How can these 'needs and expectations' be better used as differentiated digital practices (Twining, 2021) in the contexts of lived, situated (digital) literacies (Pahl and Rowsell, 2020)?
» What is the role of the campus in your students' experience and how can you approximate it with digital delivery?	» How can a blended or hybrid experience 'deliver' an ethical, values-driven and nurturing university experience?	» How can this richer, more nuanced and 'living' understanding of multiple, situated practices rather than a singular 'experience' help you to move beyond 'delivery' to 'equitable human connections that form the foundations of human learning'? (Littlejohn, 2021).
» What opportunities does better use of digital technology offer to improve your brand differentiation?	» How can digital technology at least sustain or preferably enhance the differentiation of higher education itself for its vital role in *critical enquiry*?	» Can thinking about 'brand' shift to account for both the differentiated, living digital practices of students *and* the university as a desituated place and how the two might come together for transformative and trustworthy knowledge generation with business modelling for decolonised social justice? » Can *this* be the idea of the future university?

Useful texts

Andrews, K (2021) *The New Age of Empire: How Racism and Colonialism Still Rule the World.* London: Allen Lane.

The disconnect between techno-salvationism and higher education's obligations to decolonise knowledge and practice is sidestepped in much of the 'futuring' work covered in this chapter. While this unsettling work was the subject of Chapter 4, it is crucial to include this work in following up the book as a whole.

Helsper, E (2021) *The Digital Disconnect: The Social Causes and Consequences of Digital Inequalities.* London: Sage.

Essential recent work on how digital and social inequalities relate, offering important caveats and consequences for our work in digital spaces in higher education.

Iosad, A (2020) *Digital at the Core: A 2030 Strategy Framework for University Leaders.* [online] Available at: www.jisc.ac.uk/full-guide/digital-strategy-framework-for-university-leaders (accessed 2 June 2021).

The full version of the digital strategy framework to which critical questions have been addressed in this chapter.

Jisc (2016) *Transforming Assessment and Feedback,* 29 February 2016. [online] Available at: www.jisc.ac.uk/guides/transforming-assessment-and-feedback/feed-back (accessed 2 June 2021).

Dave White: Digital – Learning – Culture. [online] Available at: http://daveowhite.com/ (accessed 2 June 2021).

Blog from one of the 'Newman Today' panellists whose work gives this chapter its title.

Williamson, B and Hogan, A (2021) *Pandemic Privatisation in Higher Education: Edtech & University Reform.* Education International (EI) Research.

Identifies key issues from mapping developments during the pandemic, including governance by technology infrastructures; programmed pedagogic environments; datafication; and surveillance.

References

Alberda, A (2020) Covid-19: Data Literacy is for Everyone. *The Nightingale: Journal of the Data Visualisation Society*. [online] Available at: https://medium.com/nightingale/covid-19-data-literacy-is-for-everyone-46120b58cec9 (accessed 2 June 2021).

Andrews, K (2017) It's a Dangerous Fiction that One Exam Will Decolonise Oxford's History Degrees. *The Guardian*, 30 May 2017.

Andrews, K (2021) *The New Age of Empire: How Racism and Colonialism Still Rule the World*. London: Allen Lane.

Arndt, S, Bengtsen, S S, Mika, C and Nørgård, R T (2020) Spaces of Life: Transgressions in Conceptualising the World Class University. In Rider, S, Peters, M A, Hyvönen, M and Besley, T (eds) *World Class Universities. Evaluating Education: Normative Systems and Institutional Practices*. Singapore: Springer.

Arnold, L (2017) The Craft of Feedback in a Complex Ecosystem. *The Higher Education Journal of Learning and Teaching*, July 2017. [online] Available at: http://hejlt.org/article/the-craft-of-feedback-in-a-complex-ecosystem/ (accessed 2 June 2021).

Baggini, J (2018) *How the World Thinks: A Global History of Philosophy*. London: Granta.

Bali, M (2021) Self-assessment Tool (of Social Justice in your Teaching) from DISCs (Disciplines Inquiring into Societal Challenges). [online] Available at: https://onehe.org/eu-activity/self-assessment-tool-of-social-justice-in-your-teaching-from-discs-disciplines-inquiring-into-societal-challenges/ (accessed 23 June 2021).

Ball, S (1990) *Foucault and Education*. London: Routledge.

Baume, D and Brown, R (2017) *Key Ideas in Blended Learning*. SEDA Working Document.

Bayne, S et al (2020) *The Manifesto for Teaching Online*. Cambridge, MA: MIT Press.

Benn, T (2010) *Letters to My Grandchildren: Thoughts on the Future*. London: Arrow.

Bennett, P and McDougall, J (eds) (2013) *Barthes' Mythologies Today: Readings of Contemporary Culture*. New York: Routledge Research in Cultural and Media Studies.

Bennett, P and McDougall, J (eds) (2016a) *Popular Culture and the Austerity Myth: Hard Times Today*. New York: Routledge.

Bennett, P and McDougall, J (eds) (2016b) *Doing Text: Teaching Media After the Subject*. Columbia: Columbia University Press.

Bennett, P, McDougall, J and Potter, J (2020) *The Uses of Media Lite*racy. New York: Routledge Research in Media Literacy and Education.

Bennett, S (2021) *Learning Design Research*. [online] Available at: https://learningdesignresearch.wordpress.com/ (accessed 2 June 2021).

Bhabha, H (1994) *The Location of Culture*. London: Routledge.

Bollmer, G (2018) *Theorizing Digital Cultures*. London: Sage.

Bovill, C (2020) *Co-Creating Learning and Teaching: Towards Relational Pedagogy in Higher Education*. St Albans: Critical Publishing.

Bradshaw, P (2020) Ergodic Education: How to Avoid 'Shovelware' When We Teach Online. *Online Journalism*, 18 August 2020. [online] Available at: https://onlinejournalismblog.com/2020/08/18/ergodic-education-how-to-avoid-shovelware-when-we-teach-online/ (accessed 2 June 2021).

Brookfield, S (2005) *The Power of Critical Theory for Adult Learning and Teaching*. Maidenhead: McGraw-Hill.

Burnett, C and Merchant, G (2014) Points of View: Reconceptualising Literacies through an Exploration of Adult and Child Interactions in a Virtual World. *Journal of Research in Reading*, 37: 36–50.

Burnett, C, Merchant, G and Guest, I (2021) Destabilising Data: The Use of Creative Data Visualtisation to Generate Professional Dialogue. *British Educational Research Journal*, 47(1): 105–27.

Campbell, L (2020) *Leap Into Action: Critical Performative Pedagogies in Art & Design Education.* London: Peter Lang.

Campione, J C (1989) Assisted Assessment: A Taxonomy of Approaches and an Outline of Strengths and Weaknesses. Journal of Learning Disabilities, 22(3): 151–65.

Carless, D (2020) From Teacher Transmission of Information to Student Feedback Literacy: Activating the Learner Role in Feedback Processes. *Active Learning in Higher Education*. [online] Available at: https://doi.org/10.1177/1469787420945845 (accessed 2 June 2021).

Carless, D (2021) *Assessment for Digital Futures*, 24 February 2021. Hong Kong: Quality Insights Digital Conference.

Carless, D, To, J, Kwan, C and Kwok, J (2020) Disciplinary Perspectives on Feedback Practices: Towards Signature Feedback Practices. *Teaching in Higher Education* (July 2020). [online] Available at: https://doi.org/10.1080/13562517.2020.1863355 (accessed 2 June 2021).

Carrigan, M (2020) We Need to Talk about Zoom. *The Post-Pandemic University*, 5 September 2020. [online] Available at: https://postpandemicuniversity.net/2020/09/05/we-need-to-talk-about-zoom/ (accessed 2 June 2021).

Coates, T (2015) *Between the World and Me*. Melbourne: Text Publishing.

Collier, D and Rowsell, J (2020) Knowing: The Literacies of Digital and NonDigital Spaces. In Pahl, K and Rowsell, J, with Collier, D, Pool, S, Rasool, Z and Trzecak, T (eds) *Living Literacies: Re-thinking Literacy Research and Practice through the Everyday*. Cambridge, MA: MIT Press.

Cook-Sather, A (2014) Student-Faculty Partnership in Explorations of Pedagogical Practice: A Threshold Concept in Academic Development. *International Journal for Academic Development,* 19(3): 186–98.

Couldry, N (2019) *Media: Why it Matters*. Cambridge: Polity Press.

Crisp, E (2020) Leveraging Feedback Experiences in Online Learning. *Educause Review*, 1 June 2020. [online] Available at: https://er.educause.edu/articles/2020/6/leveraging-feedback-experiences-in-online-learning (accessed 2 June 2021).

Crook, A and Crook, T (2020) 6 Tips for Teaching Online and in Person. *Inside Higher Education*, 26 August 2020.

Curtis, A (2021) *Can't Get You Out of My Head*. London: BBC.

D'Cruz, D (2021) 3 or 4 Things I Know about the Audio-Visual Essay or the Pedagogical Perils of Constructive Alignment. *Media Practice and Education*, 22(1): 61–72.

Daniels, H (ed) (1996) *An Introduction to Vygotsky*. London, Routledge.

Devis-Rozental, C and Clarke, S (2020) *Humanising Higher Education: A Positive Approach to Enhancing Wellbeing*. Basingstoke: Palgrave MacMillan.

Dezuanni, M (2015) The Building Blocks of Digital Media Literacy: Socio-Material Participation and the Production of Media Knowledge. *Journal of Curriculum Studies*, 47: 416–39.

Digital Education Leeds (2020) *Physical Theatre: Exploring the Slap*. [online] Available at: https://digitaleducation.leeds.ac.uk/wp-content/uploads/sites/14/2020/05/Physical_Theatre_Exploring_the_Slap_Online_Teacher_Pack-2.pdf (accessed 2 June 2021).

Doughty, R (2021) Online Learning: Long-Term Trends Accelerated by Covid-19. *The Guardian*, 16 February 2021.

Douglas, J (2017) The Struggle to Find a Voice on Black Women's Health: Front he Personal to the Political. In Gabriel, D and Tate, S (eds) *Inside the Ivory Tower: Narratives of Women of Colour Surviving and Thriving in British Academia*. London: Trentham Books.

Fanon, F (1963) *The Wretched of the Earth*. New York: Grove Weidenfeld.

Farnell, A (2021) We Can't Teach in a Digital Dystopia. *Times Higher Education*, 4 March 2021.

Filimonau, V, Archer, D, Bellamy, L, Smith, M and Wintrip, R (2021) The Carbon Footprint of a UK University during the COVID-19 Lockdown. *Science of the Total Environment*. [online] Available at: https://doi.org/10.1016/j.scitotenv.2020.143964 (accessed 2 June 2021).

Fowler, C and Redmond, S (2021) The Audio-Visual Essay as Creative Practice in Teaching and Research: Theories, Methods, Case Studies. *Media Practice and Education*, 22(1): 1–4.

Freire, P (1970) *Pedagogy of the Oppressed*. New York: Continuum.

Freire, P (1973) *Education: The Practice of Freedom*. London: Writers and Readers Publishing Co-operative.

Gabriel, D (2017) Pedagogies of Social Justice and Cultural Democracy in Media Higher Education. *Media Education Research Journal*, 8(1): 35–48.

Gabriel, D (2019) Enhancing Higher Education Practice Throught the 3D Pedagogy Through the 3D Pedagogy Framework to Decolonise, Democratize and Diversify the Curriculum. *International Journal of Technology and Inclusive Education* 8(2): 1459–66.

Gabriel, D (2020) *Transforming the Ivory Tower: Models for Gender Equality and Social Justice.* London: UCL IoE Press/Trentham Books.

Gabriel, D with McDougall, J (2020) Can We Talk? A White, Middle Class Male's Perspective on *Transforming the Ivory Tower: Models for Gender Equality & Social Justice*, Through the Black Feminist Approach of Participatory Witnessing. *Media Practice and Education*, 21(3).

Geoghegan, P (2020) *Democracy for Sale: Dark Money and Dirty Politics*. London: Head of Zeus.

Giroux, H (1988) *Teachers as Intellectuals: Toward a Critical Pedagogy of Learning*. Connecticut: Praeger.

Gourlay, L (2020) There Is No 'Virtual Learning': The Materiality of Digital Education. *Journal of New Approaches in Educational Research,* 10(1): 57–66.

Gutierrez, K (2008) Developing a Sociocultural Literacy in the Third Space. *Reading Research Quarterly,* 43: 148–64.

Hamilton, M, Heydon, R, Hibbert, K and Stooke, R (eds) (2015) *Negotiating Spaces for Literacy Learning: Multimodality and Governmentality.* London: Bloomsbury.

Harvey, D (2005) *A Brief History of Neoliberalism* (pp 36–8). Oxford: Oxford University Press.

Haw Hamburg (2020) World Sustainable Development Teach-In Day. [online] Available at: www.haw-hamburg.de/en/university/newsroom/news-details/news/news/show/4th-december-2020-world-sustainable-development-teach-in-day-2020 (accessed 22 June 2021).

Hawley, D, McDougall, J, Potter, J and Wilkinson, P (2019) Students as Partners in Third Spaces. *International Journal of Students as Partners*, 3(1).

Helsper, E (2021) *The Digital Disconnect: The Social Causes and Consequences of Digital Inequalities*. London: Sage.

Hoggart, R (1957) *The Uses of Literacy*. London: Chatto & Windus.

Holley, D (2021) Digital Learning: Pivoting to Creativity. Association for Learning Development in Higher Education. [online] Available at: https://aldinhe.ac.uk/digital-literacy/take5-54-digital-learning-pivoting-to-creativity (accessed 22 June 2021).

Hooks, B (1994) *Teaching to Transgress: Education as the Practice of Freedom*. New York: Routledge.

Hung, S-T A (2016) Enhancing Feedback Provision through Multimodal Video Technology. *Computers & Education,* 98: 90–101.

Iosad, A (2020) *Digital at the Core: A 2030 Strategy Framework for University Leaders*. [online] Available at: www.jisc.ac.uk/full-guide/digital-strategy-framework-for-university-leaders (accessed 2 June 2021).

Ishiguro, K (2021) *Klara and the Sun*. London: Faber and Faber.

Jensen, K and Bennett, E (2016) Enhancing Teaching and Learning through Dialogue: A Student and Staff Partnership Model. *International Journal of Academic Development*, 21(1): 41–53.

Jisc (2016) *Transforming Assessment and Feedback*, 29 February 2016. [online] Available at: www.jisc. ac.uk/guides/transforming-assessment-and-feedback/feedback (accessed 22 June 2021).

Jisc (2020a) *Building a Better Future*. [online] Available at: www.jisc.ac.uk/news/building-a-better-future-01-dec-2020 (accessed 22 June 2021).

Jisc (2020b) *Learning and Teaching Reminagined: A New Dawn for Higher Education?* [online] Available at: https://repository.jisc.ac.uk/8150/1/learning-and-teaching-reimagined-a-new-dawn-for-higher-education.pdf (accessed 22 June 2021).

Jisc (2020c) *Digital Pedagogy Toolkit*. [online] Available at: https://www.jisc.ac.uk/guides/digital-pedagogy-toolkit (accessed 22 June 2021).

Jones, S, Dawkins, S and McDougall, J (forthcoming, 2022) *Understanding Virtual Reality: Challenging Perspectives for Media Literacy*. New York: Routledge Research in Media Literacy and Education.

Kavenna, J (2019) *Zed*. London: Faber and Faber.

Kehler, A, Verwoord, R and Smith, H (2017) We are the Process: Reflections on the Underestimation of Power in Students as Partners in Practice. *International Journal for Students as Partners*, 1(1).

Kitsos, R (2020) Can You Teach Dance Remotely? *Simon Fraser University News*, 17 November 2020. [online] Available at: www.sfu.ca/cee/news/can-you-teach-dance-remotely.html (accessed 2 June 2021).

Kolbert, E (2021) *Under a White Sky: The Nature of the Future*. London: Vintage.

Kwhali, J (2017) The Accidental Academic. In Gabriel, D and Tate, S A (eds) *Inside the Ivory Tower: Narratives of Women of Colour Surviving and Thriving in British Academia*. London: Trentham Books.

Lancel, L and Maat, H (2021) *Touch My Touch*. Up Projects. [online] Available at: https://upprojects.com/projects/touch-my-touch/ (accessed 2 June 2021).

Landow, G (1996) Newman and an Electronic University. In Turner, F (ed) *John Henry Newman: The Idea of a University*. New York: Yale University Press.

Latour, B (2005) *Reassembling the Social: An Introduction to Actor-Network-Theory*. Oxford: Oxford University Press.

Law, J (2004) *After Method: Mess in Social Science Research*. London: Routledge.

Lawrence, J (2021) DIY Learning Analytics: Using Data to Improve Online Teaching. *Times Higher Education*, 4 March 2021.

Littlejohn, A (2021) *Seeking and Sending Signals: Remodelling Teaching Practice During the Covid-19 Crisis*. [online] Available at: https://pesaagora.com/access/seeking-and-sending-signals/ (accessed 2 June 2021).

Liu, C (2018) Social Media as a Student Response System: New Evidence on Learning Impact. *Research in Learning Technology*, 26: 1–29.

Livingstone, S and Blum-Ross, A (2020) *Parenting for a Digital Future: How Hopes and Fears about Technology Shape Children's Lives*. Oxford: Oxford University Press.

Livingstone, S and Sefton-Green, J (2016) *The Class: Living and Learning in a Digital Age*. New York: New York University Press.

Lyotard, J (1994) *The Differend: Phrases in Dispute*. Manchester: Manchester University Press.

Maguire, D, Dale, L and Pauli, M (2020) *Learning and Teaching Reimagined: A New Dawn for Higher Education?* London: Jisc.

Mahoney, P, Macfarlane, S and Ajjawi, R (2019) A Qualitative Synthesis of Video Feedback in Higher Education. *Teaching in Higher Education*, 24(2): 157–79.

Manovich, L (1999) *The Language of New Media*. Massachusetts: MIT Press.

Martin, L (2020) *Foundations for Good Practice: The Student Experience of Online Learning in Australian Higher Education during the COVID-19 Pandemic*. Australia: Tertiary Education Quality and Standards Agency.

Mayer, M (2021) *Is Transformative Learning Possible in Neoliberal Post 92 Higher Education in the UK?* Bournemouth: Bournemouth University Ed D thesis.

McBrien, J L, Cheng, R and Jones, P (2009) Virtual Spaces: Employing a Synchronous Online Classroom to Facilitate Student Engagement in Online Learning. *The International Review of Research in Open and Distance Learning*, 10(3): 1–17.

McDougall, J (2015) Open to Disruption: Education 'Either/and' Media Practice. *Journal of Media Practice* 16(1): 1–7.

McDougall, J, Walker, A and Kendall, A (2006) Shaping Up? Three Acts of Education Studies as Textual Critique. *International Studies in Sociology of Education*, 16(2): 159–73.

McGoey, L (2019) *The Unknowers: How Strategic Ignorance Rules the World*. London: Zed Books.

McKie, J (2021) Online Exams: Is Technology or Authentic Assessment the Answer? *Times Higher Education*, 28 January 2021.

McLean, J (2021) 'Gives a Physical Sense, Almost': Using Immersive Media to Build Decolonial Moments in HE for Radical Citizenship. *Digital Culture and Education*, 13(1): 1–19.

Mertala, P (2020) Data (Il)literacy Education as a Hidden Curriculum of the Datafication of Education. *Journal of Media Literacy Education,* 12(3): 30–42.

Mihai, A (2020) What's Your Story? *The Educationalist*, 28 August 2020.

Mihai, A (2021a) Are You (Really) There? Building Teacher Presence in Online Environments. *The Educationalist*, 13 January 2021.

Mihai, A (2021b) Let's Talk about Feedback. *The Educationalist*, 1 February 2021.

Mills, K and Comber, B (2013) Space, Place, and Power: The Spatial Turn in Literacy Research. In Hall, K, Moll, L, Cremin, T and Comber, B (eds) *International Handbook of Research on Children's Literacy, Learning and Culture* (pp 412–23). Oxford: John Wiley & Sons.

Moore, M (1997) Theory of transactional distance. In Keegan, D (ed) *Theoretical Principles of Distance Education* (pp 22–38). London: Routledge.

Morris, R (2021) A Reflection on Teaching Online in the Pandemic. *Teach Learn Digital*. [online] Available at: https://teachlearn.digital/?p=3678 (accessed 23 June 2021).

Naughton, J (2021) Universities Need to Wise Up – or Risk Being Consigned to History. *The Observer*, 13 February 2021.

Newman, J (1996) *The Idea of a University*. New Haven: Yale University Press.

Ng'ambi, D and Bozalek, V (2015) Special Issue on Massive Open Online Courses (MOOCs) – 'Disrupting' Teaching and Learning in Higher Education. *British Journal of Educational Technology*, 46(3): 451–4.

Nieminen, J, Tai, J, Boud, D and Henderson, M (2021) Student Agency in Feedback: Beyond the Individual. *Assessment & Evaluation in Higher Education*. DOI: 10.1080/02602938.2021.1887080

Nordmann E, et al (2020) Ten Simple Rules for Supporting a Temporary Online Pivot in Higher Education. *PLoS Computational Biology,* 16(10). [online] Available at: https://doi.org/10.1371/journal.pcbi.1008242 (accessed 23 June 2021).

Nyamnjoh, F (2017) Incompleteness: Frontier Africa and the Currency of Conviviality. *Journal of Asian and African Studies*, 52(3): 253–70. DOI: 10.1177/0021909615580867

O'Connor, M (2020) Higher Education Needs a User Experience Overhaul. *Times Higher Education*, 30 August 2020.

Onwuegbuzie, A (2002) Why Can't We All Get Along? Towards a Framework for Unifying Research Paradigms. *Education*, 122(3): 518–31.

Oomen, J, Hoffman, J and Hajer, M (2021) Techniques of Futuring: On How Imagined Futures Become Socially Performative. *European Journal of Social Theory*, 1–19.

Pahl, K and Rowsell, J, with Collier, D, Pool, S, Rasool, Z and Trzecak, T (2020) *Living Literacies: Re-thinking Literacy Research and Practice Through the Everyday*. Massachusetts: MIT Press.

Patton, L D and Bondi, S (2015) Nice White Men or Social Justice Allies? Using Critical Race Theory to Examine How White Male Faculty and Administrators Engage in Ally Work. *Race Ethnicity and Education*, 18(4): 488–514.

Peim, N (2016) The Myth of Education. In Bennett, P and McDougall, J (eds) *Barthes' Mythologies Today: Readings in Contemporary Culture*, 2nd edition. New York: Routledge.

Potter, J and McDougall, J (2016) *Digital Culture, Media and Education: Theorising Third Space Literacies*. Basingstoke: Palgrave MacMillan.

Prensky, M (2010) *Teaching Digital Natives: Partnering for Real Learning*. New York: Corwin.

Quality Assurance Agency (2020) *Building a Taxonomy for Digital Learning*.

Rancière, J (1991) *The Ignorant Schoolmaster: Five Lessons in Intellectual Emancipation*. Stanford: Stanford University Press.

Ridley, D (2016) The Empancipated Classroom. *Post-16 Educator*, 83: 9–11.

Rowntree, D (1977) *Assessing Students: How Shall We Know Them?* London: Harper Row.

Rushkoff, D (2019) *Team Human*. New York: W W Norton.

Salmon, G (2013) *E-tivities: The Key to Active Online Learning*. London: Routledge.

Samuels, R (2016) *Psychoanalyzing the Left and Right after Donald Trump: Conservatism, Liberalism, and Neoliberal Populisms*. Basingstoke: Palgrave MacMillan.

Sanders, R (2020) *Are You Resilient Enough for COVID-19?* British Educational Studies Association (BESA). [online] Available at: https://educationstudies.org.uk/blog-post-are-you-resilient-enough-for-covid-19/ (accessed 10 September 2020).

Selwyn, N (2016) *Is Technology Good for Education?* London: Wiley.

Sen, A K (2008) Capability and Well-Being. In Hausman, D M (ed) *The Philosophy of Economics* (3rd edition, pp 270–93). Cambridge: Cambridge University Press.

Spiegel, S, Gray, H, Bompani, B and Smith, J (2017) Decolonising Online Development Studies? Emancipatory Aspirations and Critical Reflections – A Case Study. *Third World Quarterly*, 38(2): 270–90. DOI: 10.1080/01436597.2016.1256767

Stommel, J, Friend, C and Morris, S (eds) (2020) *Critical Digital Pedagogy: A Collection*. Washington, DC: Hybrid Pedagogy Inc.

Swauger, S (2020) Our Bodies Encoded: Algorithmic Test Proctoring in Higher Education. In Stommel, J, Friend, C and Morris, S (eds) *Critical Digital Pedagogy: A Collection*. Washington, DC: Hybrid Pedagogy Inc.

Tait, A (2013) Distance and E-Learning, Social Justice, and Development: The Relevance of Capability Approaches to the Mission of Open Universities. *International Review of Research in Open and Distance Learning*, 14(4): 1–18.

THE Connect/D2L *Creating the Universities of the Future Today: Entering the Next Phase of Digital Transformation*, Webinar. [online] Available at: www.youtube.com/watch?v=-ND21a1cJ_E&list=PLEEwOL j3o40EVPXsehsVfo6GXmjxGX9xF&index=3 (accessed 4 February 2021).

Thomas, D and Jivraj, S (eds) (2020) *Towards Decolonising the University: A Kaleidoscope for Empowered Action*. Oxford: Counterpress.

Thomas, H (2020) *What are Learning Theories and Why are They Important for Learning Design?* [online] Available at: www.mybrainisopen.net/learning-theories-and-learning-design/ (accessed 3 February 2021).

Trenholm, R (2021) Coded Bias Review: Eye-opening Netflix Doc Faces up to Racist Technology. *C/Net*, 31 March 2021. [online] Available at: www.cnet.com/news/coded-bias-review-eye-opening-netflix-documentary-faces-up-to-racist-tech/ (accessed 2 June 2021).

Trowler, P and Trowler, V (2010) *Case Studies of Student Engagement*. York: Higher Education Academy.

Tuhiwai-Smith, L (2012) *Decolonizing Methodologies: Research and Indigenous Peoples*. London: Zed Books.

Twining, P (2021) Making Sense of Young People's Digital Practices in Informal Contexts: The Digital Practice Framework. *British Journal of Educational Technology*, 52(1): 461–81.

University of Kent (2020) *Kaleidoscope Network: Decolonising the University*. [online] Available at: https://research.kent.ac.uk/sergj/kaleidoscope-network-decolonising-the-university/ (accessed 2 June 2021).

University of Wisconsin–Oshkosh (2020) *Anti-Racist and Inclusive Online Teaching during the Racial Justice Uprisings and the Pandemic*. Center for Excellence in Teaching and Learning. [online] Available at: https://www.uwosh.edu/cetl/professional-development/instructional-development-training-online-initiative/facilitating-an-online-class/anti-racist-and-inclusive-online-teaching-during-the-racial-justice-uprisings-and-the-pandemic (accessed 1 July 2021).

Van Mourik Broekman, P, Hall, G, Byfield, T, Hides, S and Worthington, S (2014) *Open Education*: *A Study in Disruption*. London: Rowman and Littelfield.

Virti (2020) Immersive Stories and Engaging Audiences with Dr Sarah Jones. [online] Available at: https://virti.com/resources/podcast/immersive-stories-and-engaging-audiences-with-dr-sarah-jones (accessed 23 June 2021).

Vygotsky, L S (1978) *Mind in Society*. Cambridge: Harvard University Press.

Waight, S and Holley, D (2020) Digital Competence Frameworks: Their Role in Enhancing Digital Wellbeing in Nursing Curricula. In Devis-Rozental, C and Clarke, S (eds) *Humanising Higher Education: A Positive Approach to Enhancing Wellbeing* (pp 125–44). Basingstoke: Palgrave MacMillan.

Wardle, C and Derakhshan, H (2017) *Information Disorder Toward an Interdisciplinary Framework for Research and Policymaking*. Strasbourg: Council of Europe.

Weller, S and Kandiko Howson, C (2014) *Students as Co-Developers of Learning and Teaching: Redefining Expertise and Student Voice Through Student Participation in Professional Development*. SRHE Research Scoping Study. London: Society for Research into Higher Education.

White, D (2020) *Digital – Learning – Culture*. [online] Available at: http://daveowhite.com/ (accessed 2 June 2021).

Williams, R (1963) *Culture and Society*. Harmondsworth: Penguin.

Williamson, B (2016) Digital Education Governance: Data Visualization, Predictive Analytics, and 'Real-Time' Policy Instruments. *Journal of Education Policy*, 31(2): 123–41.

Williamson, B, Eynon, R and Potter, J (2020) Pandemic Politics, Pedagogies and Practices: Digital Technologies and Distance Education During the Coronavirus Emergency. *Learning, Media and Technology*, 45(2): 107–14.

Williamson, B and Hogan, A (2021) *Pandemic Privatisation in Higher Education: Edtech & University Reform*. Education International (EI) Research.

Index